Boards Under Crisis

Board action under pressure

Boards Under Crisis

Alberto Lavín Fernández
Carmelo Mazza

First published 2014 by
PALGRAVE MACMILLAN

Palgrave Macmillan in the UK is an imprint of Macmillan Publishers Limited,
registered in England, company number 785998, of Houndmills, Basingstoke,
Hampshire RG21 6XS.

Palgrave Macmillan in the US is a division of St Martin's Press LLC,
175 Fifth Avenue, New York, NY 10010.

Palgrave Macmillan is the global academic imprint of the above companies
and has companies and representatives throughout the world.

Palgrave® and Macmillan® are registered trademarks in the United States,
the United Kingdom, Europe and other countries.

ISBN 978–1–137–37921–4

This book is printed on paper suitable for recycling and made from fully
managed and sustained forest sources. Logging, pulping and manufacturing
processes are expected to conform to the environmental regulations of the
country of origin.

A catalogue record for this book is available from the British Library.

A catalog record for this book is available from the Library of Congress.

Typeset by MPS Limited, Chennai, India.

To Marta, with love

To my beloved Angela

Contents

Figures and Tables

╱ Figures

╱ Tables

Acknowledgments

This book is the end result of a research plan we wrote in 2009 to frame a doctoral dissertation for IE Business School's Doctorate in Business Administration (DBA). The plan lay at the crossroads of our respective interests as a DBA student (strategy-making and top management teams) and as a thesis supervisor (organization theory). Not surprisingly, that research plan has, day after day, focused our thoughts on the global economic and financial crisis that hit our home countries of Spain and Italy particularly hard. The fact that we are from these two countries has enabled us to see how the crisis became deeper and deeper. Our daily observations of its effects on the economy and society were some of the first sources of inspiration for writing this book. At the same time, our own curiosity about the role top management teams took during crisis—fed by our common background in management consulting—completed the motivation to write this book.

Besides these personal contextual drivers, we benefited greatly from the encouragement and endorsement received from the PhD/DBA management team at IE Business School. After providing outstanding courses, they supported us throughout the whole writing process. We wish to thank in particular Miguel Angel Díaz, Elena Revilla and Laura Maguire from the PhD/DBA Program Office for their ongoing support.

The IE Business School has provided an excellent environment for research and teaching; in our case, we also took advantage of the school's partnership with Palgrave to contribute to this book series on managerial issues. We feel deeply honored that our volume is part of the series, and we wish to thank all the people we worked with during the publishing process, starting with Cynthia Fernández (from IE Publishing) and Professor Francisco López Lubián, who revised initial versions of the manuscript, together with the sponsorship from Professor Marco Trombetta (IE's Vice-Dean of Research). We wish to particularly thank here Tamsine O'Riordan and Josephine Taylor from Palgrave Macmillan, who endlessly tried to add discipline to our writing effort in the middle of many competing consulting and teaching assignments.

Besides an in-depth review of management literature, this book largely builds upon personal contacts and interviews with board members. We wish to thank here all those who shared their knowledge, who will remain fully anonymous throughout the book, and those who helped us in the collection and interpretation of data.

We feel here the urge to warmly thank all the doctoral committee members who provided us with invaluable comments on the doctoral dissertation the book was initially based upon. Their views have largely shaped our research framework. In particular, we wish to thank Marc Ventresca for his insightful comments on organizational approaches to decision-making, Carl J. Kock for his thorough attention to reinforcing rigor in research methodology, Julio De Castro for his always lively and deep remarks on corporate governance and José Luis Alvarez, who, besides his long academic and personal friendship with one of the authors starting from PhD dissertation supervision (too many years ago now), thoughtfully took charge of commenting upon early drafts. We also wish to thank Candace Jones, whose comments in the very early stage of our research proved very fruitful, even during the final writing of the book.

We have benefitted from collaboration with many other people to finalize this book. We would like here to thank the influence of all those we met in our experience as student and professor at IE Business School. In particular, we wish to thank Dean Santiago Iñiguez de Onzoño for his encouragement.

Madrid has been a wonderful venue to discuss the early stages of this book project. How can we forget the huge number of coffee bars and restaurants where the book first took shape, and the several lunches and dinners that helped us develop the main ideas? We would also like to thank all those waiters and customers who listened to the flow of our half-articulated and often strange ideas, while eating and drinking.

Of course, we will harvest the benefits of this project, while our families have paid the highest price, bearing with sweetness and smiles our never-ending daylight telephone calls and nocturnal Skype discussions on the most unintelligible topics. We wholeheartedly thank Angela, Gianluigi, Marta, Alberto Jr, Marta Jr and Ana for their patience and devotion, and for supporting us and tolerating our continuing oscillation (typical of most writing enterprises) between frustration and excitement.

If, despite this impressive array of collaboration and support, flaws are still present in the book, the fault and responsibility remain entirely our own.

This book is the outcome of a bet with no losers: the payout was to be a dinner at Juan María Arzak's restaurant in Donostia celebrating our common love for Basque cuisine. We are there now, writing these acknowledgments.

Foreword

Board Effectiveness in a crisis

We live in interesting times. The extended global economic crisis has been with us since 2008 and businesses across the world have had to adapt to what has been described as 'the new normal'. This new normal is characterized by lower overall growth rates, the rise of new economic powers in a more multipolar world and continuing volatility. The boards and management teams of all organizations have had to learn to operate against a backdrop of a general ongoing crisis, as well as to respond to any specific crises which have afflicted their industry or business.

That this environment has put pressure on boards and CEOs and challenged the old ways of working which developed during the relatively benign global business environment of the previous decade or so, is clear. This timely book is designed to help us understand better the nature of these challenges, to analyze the key differences and chart the approaches to be taken to derive better business outcomes.

The research has drawn upon the views of many key business leaders and one is struck by what the authors have described as the general 'skeptical' perspective on board performance under pressure that has emerged. The truth from my long experience of working with organizations in these situations is very much in line with these findings and, as such, the value from exploring this area is evident.

The research asks some fundamental questions about the ability of boards to recognize that they are facing a crisis and also about the reality of meaningful decision-making at this level of the organization. The truth is that boards are often not the repositories of wisdom, global awareness and mature judgment that one hopes. These weaknesses have been exacerbated by the genuine expansion in the breadth of the world that now needs to be known and understood and the increased regulatory and stakeholder pressures on performance which board members face.

It is no surprise that board members are skeptical about their performance. The role of the board in relation to the day-to-day management of the enterprise is both strange and strained. They are expected to fulfill heavier and heavier regulatory oversight, while only engaging with the business on an irregular and limited basis. Even when things are going well, there can be frustration about the depth of debate and access to strategic discussions with the top team. As the pressure comes on, the sporadic and superficial nature of most board interactions provides little value when more serious dialogue is necessary. They may be compelled to make sudden decisions on major cost-reduction and workforce actions, shut down investment programmes or even oversee the removal of the leadership team. This all happens with the majority of board members lacking the knowledge of the business or the wider context to know if they are making the right calls. That they often get it wrong is a natural consequence of the dislocation from the core of the operations.

It is clear that there is a vast spectrum of quality in boards and especially the quality of the relationship between the board and the CEO/management team and the wider business. The trend towards truly independent directors which is explored in the book can lead to more disjointed and distant board personnel and less awareness of what really makes the business tick. This can be a truly catastrophic situation when insight and decisiveness are at a premium in difficult times. There are also some very important ideas relating to strategic alignment and shared sense of the direction of the organization which are critical to enable joined-up thinking and effective direction of the enterprise.

There is evidence that risk aversion and a tendency towards more short-term actions characterize both boards and CEOs as they come under pressure. I remember how in the aftermath of the 2008 crisis those offerings of Accenture Management Consulting that were targeted at cost reduction became the only conversation that C-suite executives wanted to have. It was also true that the best companies retained a more long-term and growth-oriented approach in parallel and took advantage of the fact that other, less strong players were caught 'like deer in the headlights'.

The boards of these weaker companies were guilty of a knee-jerk safety-first response born out of lack of confidence and inability to pull together and shape adaptive strategies under pressure. As CEOs cast around for solutions and needed to be seen to be 'doing something' it was relatively rare to see boards truly standing behind the back of their top management teams and bringing the steadying influence of a longer-term and bigger-picture perspective. Risk management and compliance were often easier paths to follow, especially when encouraged by regulators.

The other dynamic that played out in this crisis in a unique way was the emergence of new competitive forces from the developing markets in the world. These new players had the confidence of stronger domestic markets and the momentum of rapid growth from smaller initial bases. They were often also not hide-bound by the traditional board models of Western companies. Whether it was family structures, or peri-statal models, they were able to display a fleetness of foot, investment confidence and level of innovation which made them more effective both in their dealings with each other's emerging markets but also in placing competitive footholds in the developed world.

The challenges of centralization of control, short-termism and parochialism which the authors outline in this book often closed the eyes of boards, if not to the potential of playing in the multipolar world, but certainly to placing the kinds of bets necessary to engage and win.

Personalities do matter and the dynamics between the CEO and the board and between board members that is so thoroughly examined here are key. I have seen how either an over-strong CEO or an over-weak CEO in relation to the rest of the board can lead to a poor response to tough times. It can be hard for a board that has not had to exercise its decision-making muscles, due to subservience to a long-term leader, to suddenly mobilize into effective action and challenge. Conversely, if a leader has a slavish attitude to a board comprised of big beasts, it is almost impossible for the latter to avoid making inappropriate hands-on interventions and demands.

This book describes some important ideas to help create a successful board and a successful business, which together are capable of navigating crises and turning them into opportunities. At their heart is the idea of having the right strength of starting point. Anchoring around a clear and shared business strategy and keeping that in firm sight has to be the best way to begin the interactions on the best page. The team does need to be right and I like the word 'teamness' that is suggested as a basis for selection of the right players. Of course, board membership is not something that can be pulled together in rapid-response mode. This means that nominating committees need to have a constant eye on the appropriateness of the mix of talents that they are drawing upon.

As important though, in my experience, is the need to be self-aware about the personality dynamics and checking to ensure that the necessary equanimity is likely to be in place to make the tough calls, in a thoughtful way, when crisis hits. The impact of an overall abundance or scarcity mentality can be great too and the 'collective mindfulness' described here matters. I believe that this work makes some valuable points about the value of the right routines for a board to develop. Too often the routines are about governance and fiduciary responsibility, as opposed to the regular testing of the environment and the fitness-for-purpose of the business strategy. A board and CEO need to be forever scanning the wider ecosystem and finding time in their meetings to have substantive dialogues about real risks and contingency plans, as well as opportunities. Communication is indeed key.

The real challenge for boards, however, is one of overall execution effectiveness. Although the models vary across the planet as to the precise remit of such structures, the inevitable drift towards more accountability is clear and boards are going to be more and more in the spotlight during and after moments of difficulty. They have a chance to be a genuine resource that can add real value to the fortunes of the companies they oversee, but this will not happen by accident. This book seeks to identify some of the proactive steps that can be taken by organizations to leverage this capacity in a crisis and apply this, often expensive, talent for goodness and growth. The board of a company can become a source of competitive advantage—and the world needs more companies that are capable of driving growth and value, whatever the circumstances.

Mark Foster
Former Group Chief Executive
Global Markets & Management Consulting – Accenture
Chair of International Business Leaders Forum

Introduction: The Clash of the Romance of Leadership with Real Practice during Crisis

This is a book about top managers in the boardroom. It is also a book about decision-making. Ultimately, it is about crisis. We combine these three elements because we believe they are the cornerstones needed to improve our understanding of organizations during recent years.

Life in the boardroom, particularly during periods of crisis, has been underexplored. In particular, research examining the impact of changes in external strategic contexts and conditions (e.g. environmental threats or external crises' effects on directors' characteristics and decision-making processes) has received comparatively little attention in the strategic-management literature. Moreover, most literature on crisis focuses on short, highly intense crises (e.g. the Cuban missile crisis or serious aviation disasters) rather than sustained, lengthy situations of external crisis such as the one many economies are facing currently.[1]

---

[1] This is a generalization, as there are obviously a number of countries for which growth has been relatively constant (or only temporarily affected by this crisis), such as Brazil, China or Angola, to name just a few.

It is, therefore, timely to look at how crisis is affecting key decision-making in business organizations. However, it is too early (in many places the economic crisis is not yet over) and overly difficult to look for quantitative evidence that reveals changes in the decision-making process.

Perhaps hard data would never allow us to grasp the essence of decision-making in the boardroom, which lies essentially in the interaction between board members and other relevant actors. For this reason, we preferred to get into the heart of the issue by interviewing board members. We then tried to interpret what they reported by adopting theoretical constructs rooted in relevant management literature on topics such as top management teams (TMTs) and decision-making in organizations.

To look at boards during recent years is also a way to look for signs of recovery from the current economic crisis. It is expected that recovery may come from better decisions, wiser strategic moves and sounder processes in the boardroom. The hope that boards can drive companies away from stagnation and crisis is present in public opinion and media coverage. It is, therefore, important to understand whether boards are actually developing discontinuities towards this crisis, or just reacting to environmental challenges. In other words, it is crucial to understand whether boards are actually succeeding or failing in overcoming corporate crises. It is also important to understand whether any learning is taking place at board level on how to avoid deep financial crises and their effects in the future. This is important in order to understand whether the functioning of boards is part of the problem or part of the solution.

Boards are expected to find solutions to the crisis. Nevertheless, it can be argued that decision-making processes in the boardroom are reproducing constitutive elements of the crisis (Davis, 2009).

To clarify the potential clash between expectations and actual behavior it is necessary to take a close look at corporate decisions.

Do corporate leaders make decisions?

> You want to explore decision-making in the boardroom during crisis and that's interesting. However, you should try to establish if boards actually make decisions in the first place.
>
> An international executive director

Senior teams in the business world are often idealized. They are venerated by corporate citizens, who attribute miraculous powers to their bosses. They are also idealized by society at large, often influenced by the iconography of films and mass media on the topic. There is a *vulgata* of senior teams assuming that corporate leaders have quasi-magical traits that help them achieve their goals, no matter how difficult to achieve they are. According to this image, the average CEO is some kind of Gordon Gekko,[2] filthy rich, practically almighty and on occasion unscrupulous.

The management literature consistently tells us that top executives still give rise to more oral folklore than real observation (Vancil, 1987; Pye and Pettigrew, 2005). For a long time now, folklore about corporate leaders has been presenting a romantic view of the men and women at the top (Meindl, Ehrlich and Dukerich, 1985). For instance, part of James Meindl's work analyzed an attribution perspective in which leadership is interpreted as an explanatory idea to describe organizations and performance as causal systems.

---

[2] Gordon Gekko is the fictional character played by Michael Douglas in the film *Wall Street* (1987) and its sequel *Wall Street: Money Never Sleeps* (2010).

People expect rainmaking from their leaders, since not only the general public, but also managers and employees, feel reassured and more comfortable with sound (though perhaps not fully rigorous) accounts of organizational performance. Thus it is not surprising that—particularly during times of crisis, and despite the difficulty of decision-making at board level—employees, the media and society as a whole turn their gaze to corporate leaders. They are perceived as crucial in facing the situation affecting their companies, harming employment and reducing social welfare. However, although we might like to think otherwise, observations in our academic and professional lives reveal that senior managers during times of crisis feel the same type of confusion and hassle every one of us feels. As we shall see later, during turmoil the feeling of 'losing ground under your feet' has not been uncommon among corporate leaders.

It is therefore hard to admit ambiguities in organizational life, and it is particularly tough to concede that senior leadership figures such as CEOs and top politicians do not always master a solution. Very often, the solutions at hand just do not fit the problems. Just as often, solutions for problems are simply unavailable. This is particularly alarming during times of crisis; we human beings are always in search of certainty, and want to increase our perception of having control over our environment (Conner, 1992).

Decisions made under high contextual ambiguity are the landmark of James March and the Carnegie School's investigation. We look at his main tenets, as outlined by Gavetti, Levinthal and Ocasio (2007): (a) bounded rationality, (b) the role of specialized decision-making structures, (c) the role of conflicts of interest and cooperation among organizational members and (d) routine-based behavior and learning. In particular, within this impressive theoretical enterprise, we look at the garbage-can model of choice (Cohen, March and Olsen, 1972), as an *'ante litteram* agent-based' interpretation of the decision-making process (Lomi and Harrison, 2012).[3]

The garbage-can model was intended to be applied in the realm of organized anarchies (Cohen, March and Olsen, 1972). There are three main general properties characterizing what organized anarchies are made of: (a) uncertain preferences, since organizations act according to a variety of inconsistent priorities of preference, (b) unclear technology, as organizational processes and environments are not fully understood by participants and 'trial and error', as well as pragmatism (inventions born from necessity) affects the collective output and (c) fluid participation, as participants vary in the amount of time and energy devoted to different activities, including decision-making. It is self-evident how this description does not only identify organized anarchies, but also most organizations facing internal or exogenous crisis and transformation (Eisenhardt and Zbaracki, 1992).

Of course, the garbage-can model speaks the same language as many other behavioral theories, the older ones rooted in administrative and organizational literature and the newer ones developed in the fields of economics and finance. We decided to remain as close as possible to the original conceptualization of the garbage-can model of choice as developed in Cohen, March and Olsen (1972), Cohen and March (1986), March and Weissinger-Baylon (1986), Levitt and Nass (1989) and March (1994). Application in the boardroom domain is new to the garbage-can

---

[3] Although we shall frequently talk about the garbage-can model across the book, in summary it holds that the decision-making process is more frequently the casual encounter of issues, decision situations, choices (or solutions) and decision makers, rather than a 'rationally' sequenced process. It is 'solutions looking for problems', rather than the other way around.

model (for an exception, see Levinthal, 2012) so we prefer not to stretch the genuine concepts. Moreover, we believe that the stimuli of the original theorization are still intact despite the four decades that have passed from the initial formulation, as extensively shown by Lomi and Harrison (2012) in their recent 40-year celebration of the original Cohen, March and Olsen (1972) piece.

The model suggests that when under crisis (because of the increased complexity of issues), boards will act according to principles of bounded rationality and, hence, will not explore all potential alternatives at hand, but will seek to reach satisfactory solutions rather than try to maximize opportunities. This has, as it will be later shown, potential implications on decision-making processes effectiveness, boards of directors and organizational participation and, eventually, overall organizational performance.

A significant point we want to raise here is the relevance the garbage-can model has regarding organizational decision-making during crisis. According to this conceptual representation of choice, many decision-making processes within organizations do not follow economic rationality-choice models (March, 1994). Instead, there are streams of loosely coupled issues, solutions, actors and choice opportunities. Choice opportunities flow into the organization at different paces and connect (or decouple) issues, solutions and actors based on a temporal rather than a causal logic.

In later research, some of the restrictive traits of these organized anarchies were relaxed to test applicability of the theory to a wider organizational realm. Padgett (1980) relaxed the fluid participation characteristic and applied the garbage-can model of choice to an organized bureaucracy, meant as an organized anarchy with formal participation. The conclusion holds that the anarchy paradigm could still be potentially applicable. In Padgett's (1980) words, 'relative lack of emphasis on the stable and the routine ... encourages the misperception that the organized anarchy paradigm can be usefully applied *only* [emphasis added] to highly decoupled and unorthodox organizational systems'.

Our contention here is that organized anarchies can be seen as organized systems of choice filtered through the lenses of different time perspectives. A longer time perspective seems to improve the fit with the garbage-can model, whereas a short time frame is better captured by rational and political models of choice (Eisenhardt and Zbaracki, 1992). A lengthy crisis, in comparison to a short-duration crisis, increases the variety of participants; the scope of decisions and the number of solutions also becomes larger, and hence may be more appropriately characterized as akin to a garbage-can model.

Building on that perspective, other more recent constructs to explain changes like institutional work (Lawrence and Suddaby, 2006) or behavioral integration (Hambrick, 1994) are, in a way, research efforts to introduce a specific order (see Levitt and Nass, 1992, for an attempt on how to 'put a lid on the garbage can') and logic in the board-of-directors garbage can. In other words, they are alternative perspectives to decipher the causal logic behind the apparently loosely coupled garbage-can connection between issues, choices, actors and decisions.

The loosely coupled connection underlying the garbage can generates three different decision styles. Decision by 'resolution' corresponds to the traditional problem-solving outcome. Decision by 'flight' occurs when a choice has not been made for some time and problems attached to that choice move to another choice, so when the original choice is made, it solves no problems (which are now attached to other choices). Conversely, decision by 'oversight' occurs when a new choice is made quickly—using little time and energy from decision makers—before any problem is attached to it. A consideration worth exploring here is that crisis seems like a time in which 'flight' and 'oversight' are more often used as mechanisms for decision-making, compared with times of growth and reduced external ambiguity. This pattern is suggested given the intrinsic difficulty of reaching resolution during times of crisis. Departing from Cohen, March and Olsen (1972) it can be assumed then that during times of crisis more decisions are postponed or passed on to other decision makers or used as a symbolic action, rather than as an opportunity to actually solve a problem. Nevertheless, the way decisions are actually made largely depends on the characteristics of the board members and on how they play their roles and interact within the board.

How does corporate leaders' decision-making activity affect organizations?

The question of the impact of TMT characteristics and functions on organizational behaviors and results has been a constant feature in academic research beginning with the seminal paper by Hambrick and Mason (1984) about the 'large and long' shadow of leaders' characteristics in their organizations' performance. Theory states that decision-making activity is one of the key tasks at the board level (Lorsch and MacIver, 1989; Judge and Zeithaml, 1992; Forbes and Milliken, 1999; Hillman and Dalziel, 2003). Indeed, decision-making and TMT literature has to some extent evolved together and contributed largely to the theoretical body of management thinking during the last 50 years.

Most of previous research on the TMT/boardroom topic has been related to composition and has remained largely quantitative in nature, while internal processes—notably decision-making processes—have been comparatively less studied and qualitative approaches have been less frequently used. For these reasons, our work entails qualitative enquiry of this mostly unexplored phenomenon.

While most research effort on TMTs has been comparatively done on the composition side (size of the team, tenure of their members, biographies and functional and educational backgrounds in the directorate), the exploration of the process view at the top (Pettigrew, 1992) is increasingly important, particularly to understand the idiosyncratic decision-making aspects in management activity.

Decision-making is at the heart of executive activity, at least in corporate narratives about corporate settings. This is the way executives often see themselves. A more detached (and more detailed) view will tell us later that this decision-making activity is not always as pervasive in management action. At the same time, the degrees of freedom in individual decision-making are limited by the social constraints in which decision makers are embedded (Perrow, 1986). Participation in business organizations does not necessarily produce a more rational person or drive increased economic rationality in the individual. Later, when discussing the micro-dynamics of decision-making at the top during crisis, we shall argue that the converse may prove more correct. Managers decide individually, but they simultaneously decide in relation to a social context, because we live in groups. This is not different for the organizational apex, whether we talk about the CEO or the rest of the board.

While there might be shortcuts to get to know board composition in great detail in almost any company, particularly public firms (indeed in most organized markets worldwide, the composition of boards is part of the open information that public corporations mandatorily need to communicate externally), limitation of access is keenly important for process-focused research around boards.

The process view of how boards function already has a longstanding tradition of study in management literature, despite seeing comparatively less than the composition view. Table 1.1 reports a comprehensive view of TMT/board composition literature. Table 1.2 shows a more in-depth landscape of the TMT/board process view.

However, there is not a unanimous view regarding the relative importance of composition or process in board life. Consistently, other theorists in the corporate-governance and upper-echelons area suggest that to deepen our knowledge of TMTs and boards (Hambrick and Pettigrew, 2001; Pettigrew, 2001; Paroutis and Pettigrew, 2007) we need to better understand internal processes. Conversely, Stanford's Jeffrey Pfeffer (1983) contends that process measures can be dismissed because they account for little of the variation in outcomes, while Smith *et al.* (1994) purport in their TMT demography and process work that little support was found for the pure demography model.

While both streams of thought have often been presented as conflicting with the views of top management teams, the case is that both work better together in order to find out how boards really act. Deciphering how leaders interact and work collectively seems essential to understand decision-making processes and outcomes. Across this book, we shall refer to both dimensions—composition and process—as we believe they are both useful in understanding how boards make decisions during crises. Nevertheless, this work mainly adopts a process view based on an

TABLE 1.1 Conceptualization of TMT composition literature

Dominant perspective in TMT literature	Contribution areas	Contribution topics	Representative literature
		Organizations are reflections of the values and cognitive bases of powerful actors. The central premise of upper echelons theory is that executives' experiences, values and personalities greatly influence their interpretations of the situations they face and, in turn, affect their choices.	Hambrick & Mason, 1984
		Presents the evolution of the upper echelons view summarizing later refinements to the initial theory and moderator variables such as discretion and executive job demands. Two additional elaborations to the theory stand out: intra TMT power distribution and behavioral integration. Further areas of exploration (e.g. reverse causality and endogeneity, and executive effects under different national systems).	Hambrick, 2007a
Size and composition diversity are often seen as positively related to performance, with some significant exceptions	**Composition diversity and several measures of performance**	Results indicate that more innovative banks are managed by more educated teams who are diverse with respect to their functional areas of expertise.	Bantel & Jackson, 1989
		Diverse TMTs in the airline business (functional backgrounds, education and company tenure), exhibited a relatively great propensity for action, and both their actions and responses were of substantial magnitude. By contrast, they were slower in their actions and responses and less likely than homogeneous teams to respond to competitors' initiatives, but overall net effect was positive (in terms of market share).	Hambrick, Cho & Chen, 1996
		Their evidence supports the assertion that TMT dominant functional diversity is positively associated with firm performance in co-located TMTs, but negatively associated with performance for geographically distributed teams.	Cannella, Park & Lee, 2008
		In a sample of United States-based industrial firms, TMT international experience, educational heterogeneity and tenure heterogeneity were positively related to firms' global strategic postures, though functional heterogeneity exhibited a negative association.	Carpenter & Fredrickson, 2001

(continued)

TABLE 1.1 Continued

Dominant perspective in TMT literature	Contribution areas	Contribution topics	Representative literature
	TMT size and performance	Large teams and teams with less dominant CEOs were more profitable in a turbulent environment (the computer industry) than in a stable environment (natural gas distribution) consistently with information-processing variables (size and CEO dominance).	Haleblian & Finkelstein, 1993
		Demonstrated that cognitive conflict (predictor of team effectiveness) was positively related to team size and openness.	Amason & Sapienza, 1997
Size and composition diversity are often seen as positively related to performance, with some significant exceptions	**Diversity in CEO networks and performance**	Complementing research providing evidence that individual managers perform better to the extent that they interact regularly with dissimilarly-minded others; this gives a systematic consideration of factors affecting propensities to use such advice resources and that cognitive diversity of networks of CEOs seems to influence their propensity to use others and, hence, positively affect focal company performance.	McDonald, Khanna & Westphal, 2008
	Negative relationship diversity vs. performance	Contrary to mainstream theory, their findings are consistent with arguments that demographic heterogeneity may detract from team cohesiveness and agreement and negatively affect performance.	Ancona & Caldwell, 1992; O'Reilly et al.,1993

TABLE 1.2 Conceptualization of TMT process literature

Dominant perspective in TMT literature	Contribution areas	Some contribution topics	Representative literature
	Relationship between process and performance	Performance seems to be negatively related to politics at the top (best performing firms are those in which CEO shared power with the functional VPs and politics were minimal).	Eisenhardt & Bourgeois, 1988
		Job-related diversity is related to performance through internal debate.	Simons, Pelled & Smith, 1999
		Integrates the upper echelons idea with business performance through attention orientation of the top team (heterogeneity, more output function experience and shorter tenure related to attention orientation to industry change).	Cho & Hambrick, 2006
Process view is increasingly seen as promising to explain outcome, but more difficult to decipher		Introduced the power construct at the top and its sources (structural, ownership, expert, prestige) and measures.	Finkelstein, 1992
	Formalization of process constructs: power, TMT behavioral integration	Used the CEO dominance construct (and TMT size) on performance.	Haleblian & Finkelstein, 1993
		Introduced the behavioral integration TMT process.	Hambrick, 1994
		Deepened in multilevel determinants of behavioral integration.	Simsek, Veiga, Lubatkin & Dino, 2005
		Explores the relationship between behavioral integration and business performance in a service industry (positive results).	Carmeli, 2008

(continued)

TABLE 1.2 Continued

Dominant perspective in TMT literature	Contribution areas	Some contribution topics	Representative literature
	Process dynamics on the board	Introduces the roles and relationships at the top (coalitions of dyads, triads or more) of executives sharing executive power at the apex.	Alvarez & Svejenova, 2005; Alvarez, Svejenova & Vives, 2007
		Focuses on external context, internal process and time as crucial dimensions to understand board dynamics.	Pye & Pettigrew, 2005
		In a crosstalk in AME, they discuss the importance of the inner life of these leadership systems (TMTs plus boards) and agree on agenda for research (on the process and internal view of these systems).	Hambrick & Pettigrew, 2001
Process view is increasingly seen as promising to explain outcome, but more difficult to decipher	Interactions between board processes and the external environment in which they are embedded	Added to the literature on board processes through the understanding of ingratiation, interpersonal influence behaviors and board appointments.	Westphal & Stern, 2006; Westphal & Stern, 2007
		Applies the pluralistic ignorance (a herding type of behavior) and its relationship with strategic persistence in low-performance firms.	Westphal & Bednar, 2005
		Combines network research and board process to present social distancing on other boards as a control mechanism towards directors involved in corporate government changes aiming towards higher management monitoring on focal boards.	Westphal & Khanna, 2003
		This study examines whether top corporate executives may maintain more informal ties to executives of other firms in order to manage uncertainty arising from resource dependence.	Westphal, Boivie & Ming Chng, 2006

ethnographic account of people in senior positions in their decision-making settings. Despite the importance of the composition views (Hambrick and Mason, 1984, Hambrick, 2007a, Cannella, Park and Lee, 2008), we believe following Hambrick and Pettigrew (2001) and Pye and Pettigrew (2005) that a thorough description of process dynamics in the boardroom will help us better understand decision-making during times of crisis.

Boards under crisis: a summary of decision-making activity in turbulent times

Being close to the decision-making processes during times of crisis would benefit our understanding of boards' behavior. It would most likely help us better explore some areas of prescription for practitioners. This is particularly pertinent because crises are, by definition, cyclical phenomena and, therefore, we can take stock of this learning for further waves of crisis.

The perception boards have about crisis is fundamentally socially enacted (Ocasio, 1995). Despite recent intentions to measure the 'objective' intensity of crisis at the country level (MIMIC, Rose and Spiegel, 2010, 2011), it is, in general, still very difficult to 'objectify' any kind of economic adversity, particularly at the organizational/board level. So for good or bad, the intensity of crisis is also socially enacted. This has evident effects in boardroom decision-making behaviors we will try to describe across this book.

An old colleague of ours used to say in relation to perception that 'when something is perceived as real, it has actual consequences'. That is a common risk during crisis: it creates (or intensifies) spirals of pessimism (and thus, of deepened crisis) because perception usually impacts behavior (e.g. reducing expenditure or postponing or eliminating investment). As we shall argue later, this type of negative spiral has affected the corporate world, as well as society at large.[4]

This view of crisis might provide an explanation of why, regardless of the actual severity of crisis, boards react in idiosyncratic ways, probably influenced by their collective perceptions. In other words, very 'similar' boards—such as those comparable according to their composition, structure and industry—may react in very different ways under the 'same' external stimuli. There are several potential reasons behind these differences in reactions. It may be down to an executive's personality, particularly that of someone with most formal power, which is usually the CEO or chairman. Sometimes the personality of other dominant board members may impact the way the board reacts in the face of external factors. For instance, some independent or non-executive directors with high social impact or personal influence on key executives or stockholders, or (very importantly) the influence of owners or block-holders (because of their actual political and voting power at the board) may decisively influence decision-making. All these factors may sway decision-making processes in the boardroom, and ultimately impact decision content and quality.

Consequently, it is not uncommon that boards that are similar to others in principle, or in the same or comparable industries, react in very diverse ways—in very risk-averse ways in some cases and in risk-seeking, venture-prone postures in others. For example, we have seen in this research comparable companies oriented to

---

[4] Some corporate sources think that spirals of optimism (based on positive expectations) might have been partially responsible for the economic crisis and/or influenced its intensity (i.e. by causing people to ignore initial signs of crisis). According to these same accounts, analogous spirals may have lengthened the crisis.

pure cost cutting and others in similarly mature industries more oriented towards expansion and the search for new opportunities. The internal configuration of the board and cohesion among directors is also a cause of this divergence (Ocasio, 1995).

Having said that, if we admit crisis is as much 'built' as it is 'objective', the way in which crisis is observed by the board decisively affects their reaction to circumstances. For example, the mere effort of seeking unifying views in the boardroom impacts the decision-making process. There is a greater need to elaborate and interchange information, more time and energy dedicated to reach agreement when feasible and there is displacement or delay in the content of meetings or increased tension and conflict, affecting the internal teamness (Hambrick, 1998) of the board.

The mainstream quantitative exploration of boards (e.g. dimension, composition, tenure and diversity) does not fully explore some of the underlying factors explaining these behaviors. For example, for many directors crisis is perceived as a time of threat (e.g. higher risk of mistakes) or increased opportunity, and risk aversion may be exacerbated (or, on the contrary, risk might be ignored). The hazard of legal liabilities or potential threats over professional prestige may be felt more keenly, and acted upon. This likely affects the dynamics of decision-making.

The goal of this book and the research framework

This book covers four main areas of research on boards under crisis. Firstly, the analysis of crisis as a social enactment process, something very briefly discussed in the previous paragraphs. Secondly, short-termism and in which way the time-orientation focus (short vs. long term) of board decision-making may be altered by crisis as such. Crisis generally promotes increased short-termism at the board level, in part as a way to limit risk, and because of enlarged causal ambiguity in the generation of results during crisis (Mosakowki, 1997; Powell, Lovallo and Caringal, 2006). Thirdly, increased centralization and control of decision-making in the boards, which is inherent to amplified environmental uncertainty and rising perceived risk for decision makers. Executives, and boards for that matter, protect themselves by increasing the degree of control in all happening around or below them. As we shall suggest across the book, as much as this behavior may provide decision makers a greater (though often false) feeling of control, several perverse implications result from this behavior, particularly on timeliness and the cost of decision-making. Finally, the fourth area is about the increased self-interest (opportunism) and parochialism of boards under crisis. It has been suggested that crisis promotes some individualistic, purely self-serving behaviors (Freud, 1959; Weick, 1993). While we could not properly speak here of predatory behavior, we can certainly argue that crisis is a situation is which opportunism (Williamson, 1975) is accentuated, and where increased tension among parties is displayed. Several examples of such behaviors will be described across the chapters of this book. We will also discuss the managerial and business performance implications of all these behaviors during crisis.

In this book we deal with decision-making in the boardroom during crisis, building arguments and generalizations rooted on observations (Trochim and Donnelly, 2007). We follow a grounded approach (Glaser and Strauss, 1967; Locke, 2001), based mainly on in-depth interviews with board members (referred to as 'sources'). The ethnography analysis was complemented with selected secondary data (e.g. business press, market authority public information and sources' biographies and annual reports) in order to grasp the context of boardrooms beyond our sources' accounts.

We adopted a grounded theory approach as it is especially effective in analyzing 'the actual production of meanings and concepts used by social actors in real settings' (Gephart, 2004; Suddaby, 2006). The method is most suited to efforts to understand the process by which actors construct meaning out of inter-subjective experience (Suddaby, 2006). Moreover, qualitative research approaches are best suited to develop arguments and new theories (Trochim and Donnelly, 2007) when no established hypotheses are on the ground. It is thus the case for executive decision-making (Hambrick, 1995), where operationalization for quantitative methodologies is still in its infancy (Simsek *et al.*, 2005). This explains the academic community's growing advocacy towards the use of qualitative approaches (Gephart, 2004; Hambrick, 2007b; Bansal and Corley, 2011).

Qualitative exploration is an apt way to explore the inner life of boards, despite a few obstacles of observational and interview-based research on these settings. First, the answer rate within the C-executive suite for this type of research tends to be low comparable to other types of surveys (i.e. 'the 10–12 percent rate typical for mailed surveys to top executives', Hambrick, Geletkanycz and Fredrickson, 1993), and involving a great deal of data-gathering work just to obtain a significant sample size. Second, as Hambrick and Pettigrew (2001) hold, low transparency of executives in their research interaction is likely.

Despite these caveats, recent research streams contend that scientific investigation of how people make decisions begins with observation, not with testing hypotheses drawn from mathematical and statistical theories. Hence, a more ethno-methodological approach may help us understand decision-making at work (Gore, Banks, Millward and Kyriakidou, 2006). This especially applies in our research case, since the crisis period is not yet over and the time series is still incomplete, denying us the ability to perform a quantitative longitudinal study (BBVA Research, 2012).

Nevertheless, accessing the 'black box' at the top is very difficult. Due to this difficulty, despite the importance of decision-making theory (Westphal and Bednar, 2005) there is yet little systematic research on decision-making processes at the corporate boardroom level. This difficulty of accessing top managerial settings has been long acknowledged; 25 years ago Jackall (1988) mentioned this limitation in his book *Moral Mazes*, dealing with the world of corporate managers. Access was also a remarkable complication for the research leading to this volume: accessing a significant sample of insiders, both in number and relevance, was one of the most time-consuming tasks needed to accomplish this work.

Given the intrinsic difficulty in accessing boards and board members, access to sources was granted via snowball sampling. Although snowball sampling may provide lower external validity than other types of sampling (Trochim and Donnelly, 2007), we think it is the best feasible approach for this type of board research. Boards and board members form a group of their own (Hambrick, 1994; Forbes and Milliken, 1999; Paroutis and Pettigrew, 2007) with frequent and closed links among their members. For instance, among the 1000 largest US companies in 2001, the average company that shared a director could reach every other company in fewer than four steps: as Davis (2009) cogently argues: 'an airborne flu virus that infected the Enron board in January 2001 could have made its way to 650 Fortune 1000 companies by May through monthly board meetings'.

Sources selected in our research met at least one of the following three basic criteria: they (a) served as directors (chairman/executive director or external/non-executive director) at the time of the interview in at least one board of directors, (b) had at least two years' experience as directors in their current or previous companies or (c) cover a wide array of industries: energy, manufacturing, technology and communications, financial services and others.

The final sample consisted of 26 senior executives (chairmen, CEOs and external directors) representing collectively at the time of the research 42 companies with an aggregated gross revenue in excess of €300 billion at the end of 2010. Companies were mostly incorporated in Spain (78 percent) with the remaining 22 percent incorporated abroad or with dominant participation by foreign capital, mostly in continental Europe and the UK. Of those incorporated in Spain, at least one third had subsidiaries outside of Europe at the time of research.

The average age of sources at the time of the interviews was 56 years of age. Three sources were female. The interviews took place during the second half of 2011 and early 2012, expanding across a total period of approximately 35 weeks. The average duration of the interviews was 58 minutes. Approximately one fifth of the sources were interviewed two or more times to confirm interpretations.

Quotes from sources have been cleaned of anything that could lead to the identification of the interviewees. Moreover, all colloquial expressions that might be linked to specific sources have been removed or replaced with neutral or non-traceable expressions. We do not report in this book any further information on the sample, age breakdown, industry breakdown or corporate-profit breakdown, which could be used to identify companies and board members. In this way, we intend to maintain our sources' anonymity, whilst keeping intact their insights.

One of the most fundamental points of discussion in the use of interviews in qualitative research situations is the minimum sample size needed in order to reach theoretical saturation. The final sample size was defined using the process of grounded theory building described before, orienting our theoretical sampling towards reaching theoretical saturation, i.e. the condition where additional information pieces do not increase theoretical density of the account (Fetterman, 1998). Thus, given this grounded approach, there was not a planned sample size upfront, even though several sources mention that as few as six to 12 interviews may render satisfactory results depending on the characteristics of the sources (Romney, Weller and Batchelder, 1986), or the nature of the interviewing tool (Guest, Bunce and Johnson, 2006). During the interviews after theoretical saturation, we used a confirmatory approach (Fetterman, 1998) both to fill in potential gaps in the emerging model and to circumvent threats to validity.

A key approach to limit bias in this type of qualitative research (Eisenhardt and Graebner, 2007) is using numerous and highly knowledgeable sources who view the focal phenomenon from different perspectives. To increase empirical evidence validity, in addition to the interviews with senior executives, industry or corporate governance experts were also interviewed (eight interviews) during 2011 and early 2012. Sources included key officers in regulating or institutional bodies and former and current directors. Finally, we interviewed five general managers reporting to their boardrooms in five listed companies. These additional interviews were used both to confirm preliminary findings and to shed light on the relation of boards with their management teams during crisis. In addition, the content of this book is supported by dozens of interactions between the authors and other top managers and directors during the research process.

Given the multifaceted and diverse nature of boardroom activity, the profile of sources and the drawbacks associated with a standardized interviewing approach in these settings, the selected approach for research was in-depth semi-structured interviewing. Semi-structured or non-structured interviewing takes advantage of the use of open-ended questions (Fontana and Frey, 1994). Typically this type of question elicits more information, but it is often more difficult to use and requires a higher level of expertise in the researcher, as the most important piece of equipment in ethnography is the ethnographer her/himself (Fetterman, 1998, Atkinson and Hammersley, 1994). This semi-structured interviewing approach also offered us as researchers more latitude to adapt to methodological sampling using this grounded theory approach.

Grounded theory procedures to interpret data are based on iteration and the constant comparison between incidents found in the gathered data and the theoretical concepts emerging from this data (Barnes, 1996). In this study, we created conceptual categories based on the raw text in the data transcripts of the interviews, finding patterns and themes and doing some initial clustering by grouping related themes.

The first grouping of ideas based on initial interviews had almost 700 different conceptual ideas. This first coding was done on a line-by-line (or paragraph) basis, in parallel with the identification of concepts. This initial process of 'open coding' (Corbin and Strauss, 2008) was shared and discussed with two other researchers, until an agreement was reached for that initial conceptualization.

The frequency of repetition of ideas helped form the initial major categories within these groups. Then, the authors began to make contrasts and comparisons. The process included the hierarchy or grouping of some concepts (Miles and Huberman, 1994) as well as some differentiation. This process of 'axial coding' (Corbin and Strauss, 2008) conveyed the connection of themes between different categories. This second step in the grounding process was also validated with the same set of two peer researchers until an agreement was reached about the groupings.

During this stage, the research entered into more intensive iterative and comparison processes. The process at this point included not only comparison between data incidents and theory (Glaser and Strauss, 1967) but abductive processes of reasoning (Peirce, 1931; Niiniluoto, 1999; Ketokivi and Mantere, 2010; Walsh and Bartunek, 2011) to establish causal chains of inference among existing groupings or sets of ideas. This abductive process of inference is used by most management-consulting practices in problem-solving processes (Minto, 1996) and it is, ironically, the same approach to the logics of 'deduction' Niiniluoto (1999) refers to in Sherlock Holmes' practice.

In the third stage of the research, theoretical sampling became more focused (i.e. oriented to fill in the gaps in the emerging model) to validate preliminary findings (Fetterman, 1998). Thus, following Purdy and Gray (2009), interviews evolved to cover the preliminary variable model in depth. Theoretical sampling continued in parallel with the process of coding.

We considered having reached theoretical saturation after meeting 18 sources. Most of what appeared thereafter were refinements on the analysis and nuances on board behaviors, depending on industry or ownership structure. Importantly, when this grounded model was established, literature was used to supplement findings or to name theoretical constructs emerging from the grounded data, using literature as an additional source (Goulding, 1998).

Finally, the grounded theoretical model included four overarching themes; we have called them here 'aggregate theoretical

First-order codes	Second-order constructs	Aggregate theoretical dimensions
• Restrictions to credit • Depth: Demand plummeting • Scope: Most industries affected (even impact not uniform) • Length: Long crisis or new normality?	'Idiosyncratic' nature of crisis	Crisis is not univocal
• Crisis is individually or socially enacted • Reactions do not always follow 'reality' (decoupling) • Symbolism	Enactment or conscious symbolism?	
• Cost cutting activity • Working capital and cash management investment reduction • (Selective) divestiture	Use of short-term oriented tactics	Short-termism
• Less (environmental) opportunities • Lack of formal (strategy) process more visible	Worsened portfolio of strategic options	
• Reduced or postponed key investment or M&A activity • Other activity (e.g. diversification) also reduced or postponed	Reduced strategic activity	
• Centralization of information processing • Constriction in control • (Micro/mis)management and executive de-motivation	Control through exertion of CEO (or board) power	Centralization and control
• More formalized agenda of meetings • More formal recording (voting and minutes)	Formalization	
• De-layering, reduction or short-cutting intermediate decision structures • Overload for board structures and apparition of new ones	Ad hoc bureaucratization	
• Proprietary directors defending stock position and value of investment • Independent directors defending status and hedging position • Executive directors play politics to save face and protect role	Increased self-interest	Parochialism and conflict
• More complex problems and reduced slack • Increased participation (voluntary and induced)	Stronger substantive debate	
• Increased importance of voting power • Increased prominence of formal position and access to information • Other factors (e.g. large competing shareholders) intensify differences	Intensified importance of structural differences in board processes	
• Characters' clashes • Baseline mood and morale changes (e.g. depressed executives or anxious owners)	Harsher personal clashes	

FIGURE 1.1 / Analytical coding process to induce theoretical dimensions

dimensions', grouping overall findings across boardroom reactions under crisis. They included 12 conceptual categories ('second-order constructs') in the second level of grouping and 31 in the third level of grouping ('first-order codes'). A graphical representation of this final theoretical model can be found in Figure 1.1.

Outline of the book

This book is structured into seven chapters, following the logical flow shown in Figure 1.2.

We prefer to deal with short-termism and centralization first (Chapters 3–4) and then the root cause, parochialism, later (Chapter 5), as centralization and particularly short-termism are, in general, more visible outcomes. We are not suggesting here that parochialism is the only reason behind short-termism and centralization during crisis. Nevertheless, our research suggests parochial interests are a significant determinant to increased focus on the short term and centralization.

The chapters are structured as follows. In Chapter 2 we explore the aggregate theoretical dimensions, first by going beyond the

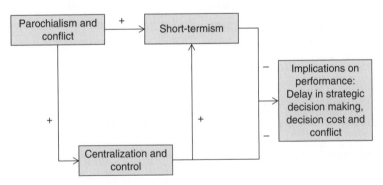

FIGURE 1.2 Main effects of crisis in the boardroom

'objective' nature of crisis and exploring in detail how perception of crisis may differ and how this can affect boardroom decision-making processes. We next shall introduce the other three dimensions derived from the interviews with our sources: short-termism, centralization and parochialism.

Chapter 3 is devoted to the exploration of increased short-termism in the boardroom during crisis. Chapter 4 covers another salient trait of crisis in boardroom decision-making: the centralization of decision-making in both facets of information-processing and actual decision-making centralization, as well as a number of performance implications of such behaviors. Chapter 5 hosts an in-depth description of the micro-dynamics of boardroom decision-making processes, characterized by increased tension, accentuated self-interest and parochialism. To do so, we will adopt the theoretical perspective based on the garbage-can model of choice (Cohen, March and Olsen, 1972).

In Chapter 6 we explore the similarities, comparisons and differences between TMTs (boards, in this case) and other critical decision-making groups (firefighters, surgical teams, judges, etc.). The goal is to complement learning about decision-making process dynamics at the top through the observation of other decision-making groups.

Finally, in Chapter 7 we suggest some areas of prescription for boardrooms in crisis, together with a number of avenues for further research on the topic that may be useful in understanding crises and their impacts upon decision-making at boardroom level.

Chapters 2, 6 and 7 blend a practitioner-oriented with an academic approach while Chapters 3, 4 and 5 follow a rather practitioner-oriented approach.

chapter **2**

The Crisis in the Boardroom, or How This Crisis is Perceived in Corporate Settings

Boardroom decision-making process during crisis is a crucial concern both from a theoretical viewpoint and a practitioner's viewpoint. Boardroom interpretation of crisis shapes current decision-making and, through this, both organizational reactions to crisis and organizational ability to perform effectively in the future and, eventually, when crisis will be left behind both at the corporate and global levels.

It can be said that the trigger for this book—even if not its essence—is the observation and interpretation of current crisis. We must therefore clarify from the outset what is meant by crisis in board settings. This contextualization is crucial in order to understand more clearly the voices from the boardroom, not least because reasoning has been characterized in management research as a context-dependent process (Ketokivi and Mantere, 2010; Weick, 1989; Golden-Biddle and Locke, 1993).

Crisis? What crisis?[1]

It has long been known that top management teams heavily affect corporate reactions (Janis, 1982; Zajac and Westphal, 1996; Graffin *et al.*, 2008). In other words, organizations shadow their leaders and this fact influences the way organizations react to their shifting immediate environment. This organizational influence of top management underscores the need to scrutinize their decision-making processes under crisis, and the fundamental decision-making group for most organizations is their board of directors.[2] In addition, regulators and media now closely scrutinize how corporations are governed, due to the eroding impact of crisis in aggregate welfare dimensions such as employment rates or public spending.

Regarding the definition and attributes of crisis, management literature has not yet made a sufficiently clear distinction between threat and a number of related terms, including crisis. Staw, Sandelands and Dutton (1981) claimed that threat ('environmental event with impending negative or harmful consequences for the entity') is a major component of most events that the term 'crisis' attempts to explain (Gladstein and Reilly, 1985).

---

[1] The title of a 1975 album by the rock band Supertramp provides an excellent heading for the beginning of this chapter. It is not the first time that such a title (or a similar one) has been used by musicians: for example, in 1933, the year of the rise of Nazism in Germany, an Italian song 'What is this crisis?', by Rodolfo De Angelis, became very popular, interpreted as a soft critique of the Fascist government.

[2] A decision-making group like this (or comparable in their responsibilities) exists not only in for-profit firms but also in non-for-profit (e.g. NGO) and political organizations; odds are that even if we are talking here mostly about business organizations, a significant part of our conclusions might be generalized to other, non-business settings.

Long-established characterization of crisis (Hermann, 1963) depicts it as having three main components: (1) it is a major threat to system survival, (2) it allows little time to react and (3) it is unanticipated. Others define crisis as: (a) a major threat to system survival (Mishra, 1996) with little time to respond (Hermann, 1963), (b) involving an ill-structured situation (Turner, 1976) and (c) where resources are inadequate to cope with the situation (Starbuck and Hedberg, 1977; Webb, 1994).

Maybe because of this reduced lead time and high-intensity characterization of crisis (Weick, 1993; Weick, 1988; Allison and Zelikow, 1999), this type of short and sudden crisis has been a main focus of investigation, while less attention has been comparatively paid to more structural or longer duration crises or environmental threats (Staw, Sandelands and Dutton, 1981; Gladstein and Reilly, 1985; Milburn, Schuler and Watman, 1983). This duration ingredient is relevant as there are no clear references in the past for crises of this dimension and length that we can benefit from in our analysis, with the only possible exception being the downturn immediately following the 1929 crash, as accounted by John Kenneth Galbraith (1954) and the sociological work of Karl Polanyi (1957).

Crises are characterized by low probability, but are highly consequential events that threaten the most fundamental goal of an organization (Weick, 1988). However, the word 'crisis' is an often overused term with a very imprecise meaning (Smart and Vertinsky, 1984). As an extreme case of this breadth of interpretation, under debate is whether the current 'crisis' should be considered as a change in paradigm (a 'new normality'[3]).

---

[3] The 'new normality' term seems to have been coined by Ian Davis, a former McKinsey managing director (2003–9).

We will refer to the current crisis as a revolutionary type of structural change, even if some of its elements, such as its duration, may also drive us in the direction of a combination of revolutionary and evolutionary changes (McKinsey, 2009a).

From the perspective of decision makers, crises occur when they *perceive* that valued interests are seriously threatened, when they *feel* uncertain that a practical response will definitely protect these interests and when they *believe* a quick response is needed (Tjosvold, 1984). Given the use of terminology (*perceive, feel, believe*) it is easy to anticipate that there is, in general, little that is purely 'objective' for decision makers about the concept of crisis. This is not surprising, as the awareness of crisis in small groups is influenced not only by the awareness of each individual, but also jointly by the members who make up the group.

This is a significant topic in this research as there is more difficulty in organizing coordinated action (in any group, but specifically in the boardroom) if (when) there is not a common perception about crisis (or even insufficient agreement about its nature in the first place), which in turn may affect unity of action and actual quality of decision.[4]

In fact, there have been (and still are) significant 'objective' dimensions characterizing crisis. Where we live, for instance, can have particular traits that differentiate our experience of crisis compared with people living in other parts of the world: in some parts of Europe, for example, the current economic crisis is

---

[4] Attention is conditioned by emotion (i.e. emotionally laden items receive more attention); and emotion affects memory (i.e. increased feeling of remembering) (see for example Sharot, Delgado and Phelps, 2004). Action (i.e. reaction to crisis events) is conditioned by this process: in plain words, it is difficult to react to something if it doesn't first catch our attention.

intense and is mostly *transversal*—affecting almost every industry and many regions—even if its intensity is also characterized by industry and geographical differences. In addition, it is proving to be very lengthy. As already mentioned, the traditional argument of crisis in TMTs is strongly related to crisis defined as short-duration events such as the Cuban missile crisis (Allison and Zelikow, 1999) or the Mann Gulch fire tragedy (Weick, 1993).[5] Thus, the length of the current crisis challenges most managerial literature.[6] As we shall see, all these particular features may have been conditioning boardroom reactions to this crisis, thus potentially affecting their effectiveness.

There is wide agreement that the opening episode for the current economic crisis (at least symbolically) was the default of Lehman Brothers on 15 September 2008 and, at the time we are writing this book (late 2013), crisis is still a key issue throughout Europe. One of our informants, with a long CEO and board member experience, describes the unique nature of the current crisis: 'I have been in top positions for a few decades now; I have never seen such a deep crisis. It is affecting everything and everywhere. I have just had today a lunch with (top) people from many

---

[5] While the Mann Gulch tragedy does not specifically touch on TMTs, it clearly illustrates what happens when organizational rules and leadership references collapse; thus it has clear direct implications for TMTs during crisis.

[6] Researchers (Milburn, Schuler and Watman, 1983) had already explored reactions in front of crisis or threat, both from the individual and organizational perspectives and from a wider, less short term oriented perspective. More recently, other related literature (Pearson and Claire, 1998) presents a profound analysis of organizational crisis and crisis management traditions, suggesting previous research on organizational crisis lacked integration and calling for a multidisciplinary approach (psychological, socio-political and technological) to research in crisis management.

industries and there is wide agreement about this [the intensity and span of the crisis].'

However, there is seldom a unified view of crisis in board settings at the individual organization level. An apparent paradox is that external economic crisis does not always and necessarily stand for crisis in the boardroom. Thus, board functioning might go unchanged, even in the face of profound external turmoil. According to a former CEO:

> There is never such a thing as bad news in the boardroom. Nothing happens. Never. If something bad has really happened, then it doesn't 'happen'. You don't speak about it. There is other discourse, other rhetoric. If things go well, then they do—and if they don't, we report that we are already taking action to solve problems and that results are on their way. Therefore, there can be a deep external crisis and the board might go unnoticed. Crisis means something different in the boardroom. Of course, it can be external economic crisis, but there is crisis when there is a situation that affects or threatens the board itself. For instance, (when there is) a hostile takeover or there are bitter arguments among key stockholders. This is the most usual crisis in the boardroom.

The chairman of another company suggests something similar: 'Crisis for the board is not (necessarily) crisis outside. It is crisis inside. Therefore, crisis intensity is contingent also on how this is *internally interpreted*, not only on how substantive it actually is' (emphasis added). The opinion from the later informant is in line with the idea that crisis is filtered through our own cognitive lenses (Weick, 1969; Simon, 1945) both as an individual and group enactment (Weick, 1988; 2010). What is a crisis to one individual or group may well not be to another (Kupperman, Wilcox and Smith, 1975; Smart and Vertinsky, 1984). Crisis is in the 'eye of the beholder'.

At the same time, and partially related to crisis perception, is the issue of the detachment between symbolic and substantive behaviors of the board of directors in the face of external crisis, an idea also latent in the earlier accounts. In the words of one of our interviewees: 'It can perfectly happen that the real situation is being affected—e.g. worsened business results—and the board acts as if nothing actually happened.'

While the boardroom provides resources and/or monitors management (Hillman and Dalziel, 2003; Johnson, Daily and Ellstrand, 1996; Zahra and Pearce, 1989) and thus should look towards the success of the organization, the preceding passages clearly suggest that during external crisis no necessarily managerial substantive action takes place and that significant symbolic action decoupled from actual policy may emerge (Westphal and Zajac, 1994; Westphal and Zajac, 1998; Westphal and Zajac, 2001). During crisis (or particularly because of it), symbolic action plays a significant role in the boardroom. Boardroom actors have corporate goals but they also have individual objectives and interests, often conflicting among them. This apparent decoupling between boardroom activity, actors' interests, evolution of the business and company stewardship has also been reported by interviewees as partially causal of the existing economic crisis situation.

An independent director puts it quite bluntly, suggesting that it is probably impossible to solve current problems and face the future, while trying to disguise previous mistakes: 'I can see no way of getting out of this crisis without changing [the composition of] boards. There were obvious mistakes before. Those who took us here cannot guide us out.' Along the same lines, the chairman of a large company asserts: 'I had a tough time to remove a number of board members on my own board. They were ageing, had many perks and basically added nothing, but they were defending their seats and benefits. Of course, oft-times you have to change people to change things ... Less reflection in the past originated to some extent this situation we live in now.' On the same topic, a long-tenured board member serving in the directorate of several listed companies, mentions contritely: 'Had we [boards] looked into things as carefully as we do now, intensity of crisis would have been much lower than it is today.'

These comments, while touching on managerial perceptions of crisis and boardroom decoupling between symbolic and actual practices, open the debate on the antecedents of crisis. This has been the object of several studies (e.g. Taylor, 2009; Foldvary, 2008; see also Davies, 2010 for an in-depth account on the origins of the current crisis). Among these investigations, very relevant for our research is the analysis by Harvard sociologists Dobbin and Jung (2010), which purported that antecedents to the current crisis situation may be related to an excessive focus on shareholder value without useful recipes for risk management.

Crisis also has substantive dimensions such as differences in performance among countries or firms. The current economic crisis has been objectively asymmetric and there have been winners and losers among almost any sample of countries, industries or companies affected by it. For example, among the developed countries only Canada had a growth rate that can be compared with some of the emergent countries in the period 2000–10. Despite this, the crisis also deeply—but more shortly—affected emergent economies (BBVA, 2011; 2012), and future global growth is expected to be primarily associated with these countries (BBVA, 2013).

However, these economic dimensions are not necessarily coupled with managerial views about crisis. As such, it can be confirmed that there is not a univocal view about crisis. The connection of the perception of crisis with strategic decision-making is thus problematic; contextual ambiguity of crisis, as described above, suggests that environment is enacted in the process—and establishing common action for a board is more difficult to agree, act upon and achieve.

For example, differences in the boardroom about the perception of the environment are more frequently voiced during crisis, particularly around topics with significant implications for survival and long-term success of the organization such as the price of oil and other raw materials, dollar exchange rates or country interest/risk premium rates. There are several types of these key uncertainties. In this research, we have identified at least two different, external environment-led categories of uncertainty: (a) global-level uncertainties with ambiguous organizational impact, and (b) global-level uncertainties with definite organizational impact.

Global-level uncertainties with a more or less general (and, thus, more ambiguous to assess) impact for organizations are those related to, for instance, US growth and prospects; the type of policies and political arrangements (e.g. the discussions about the US 'fiscal cliff'); the strength of European construction and the financial viability and risk of intervention in European countries; or the growth expectations for China, Brazil and other emerging countries. All the former are general, political or macroeconomic concerns, but their effects happen at the industry or country levels and, therefore, it is more difficult—in general—to gauge or anticipate what the effect might be at the organizational or individual firm level. However, they remain critical because of their indirect but potentially serious effect at the organizational level.

Second, there are other global uncertainties with a more direct—or, at least, clearer to assess—effect in organizations. For instance, those directly tampering with income or affecting cost at the microeconomic level (e.g. oil price, dollar evolution and exchange rates, country risk, competition, market size, to name just a few). While there is still ambiguity in those variables, their impact on organizational settings can be predicted or approximately calculated.[7] Whereas all the former may be also happening during non-crisis times and similarly influencing business results, these concerns are particularly painful during crisis because they often threaten long-term survival of the organization. For example, the CEO of a multinational corporation asserts:

> There is a lot of debate and small talk among the board about a number of macroeconomic variables these days; of those, dollar exchange rate and oil price progress are probably the most important for the majority of us. But it is beginning to be some type of betting or gambling, trying to find out its (most likely) evolution. Paradoxically, there is always a sound (ex-post) explanation to whatever the evolution has been for these variables.

This opinion reminds us of the famous quote attributed to Niels Bohr, the Danish physicist among the fathers of atomic physics, who said that 'prediction is very difficult, especially about the future'. Agreeing on how to deal with these variables is often a critical task for boards during crisis. Very often, the process to reach an agreement implies a large degree of debate and substantial devotion of boardroom time. The need to reach agreement or some common consensus about a number of issues or environmental variables (as in to establish predictions

---

[7]This division into two types of uncertainties was made for the sake of clarity; this is not to neglect that there are often interactions among both types of global uncertainties (e.g. the negotiations about the US 'fiscal cliff' may obviously affect dollar evolution).

or prepare plans) makes the process of decision-making more complex, even tense at times.

This task complexity involves information-gathering, then processing and analyzing it and, eventually, coming to a final decision. The time it takes to reach a decision is important at all times for business performance but is particularly relevant during crisis: a quick reaction may be needed. Postponement in decision-making, as we shall see, brings potentially serious implications in terms of timeliness and cost.

The implications of boards' decision-making on crisis are manifold. The interviews that we extensively mention in the next chapters point out three key traits of boards' decision-making under crisis: short-termism, centralization and parochialism/self-interest. The fuzziness in the evolution and interpretation of the different categories of external uncertainties we described earlier fosters an increased degree of short-termism at the board level. The idiosyncratic ambiguity of crisis makes the decision-making process often more centralized: those with the ultimate responsibility for decision feel the urge to increase their control over the organizational decision-making process and its outcome (Milburn, Schuler and Watman, 1983). The reduced slack that characterizes crisis makes effective decision-making more confronted against self-interest and parochialism. In the words of a CEO at a large global organization: 'There is no problem when there is abundant food on the table. The tough thing is when there is little food missing and, suddenly, the lights are turned off. This is a good metaphor for crisis. Eventually people fight more against each other.'

Short-termism and parochialism may be considered as somehow 'structurally' present in the boardroom (the former very particularly for listed firms) also in non-crisis times. Centralization is already well known in managerial literature (Cameron, Kim and Whetten, 1987; Cameron, Whetten and Kim, 1987) and is intrinsic to the nature of small groups of people in decision-making situations under pressure (Driskell and Salas, 1991). In the next section we will look in more depth at short-termism in the boardroom during crisis.

Short-term orientation and short-termism in the boardroom during crisis

Life is more difficult during times of crisis yet the pressure to deliver results is at least the same (if not more) under less manageable or predictable circumstances. The importance of short-term focus under crisis is increasing, particularly for those companies under the close scrutiny of the financial markets. As we will outline in the next chapter, short-termism takes different shapes. Many of them, in particular those determined by external variables (see Figure 2.1), are independent of crisis and very likely pre-existed. So, short-termism appears to affect boards in the same way before and during crisis, although with enlarged intensity in the case of crisis.

As investigated by the huge body of literature on rationality limitations and bounded rationality (Simon, 1945; March and Simon, 1958; March, 1994), decisions become more stressful and complex under crisis, due to cognitive limitations of decision makers becoming more salient both at the individual and boardroom levels. These limitations restrain the temporal horizon of decision. They foster a more time-bounded focus, postponing more strategic concerns. In plain terms, board members—as every one of us would probably do—concentrate on those issues producing results more easily or quickly, because of increased difficulties to

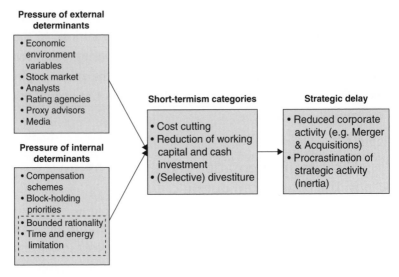

Pressure of external determinants

- Economic environment variables
- Stock market
- Analysts
- Rating agencies
- Proxy advisors
- Media

Pressure of internal determinants

- Compensation schemes
- Block-holding priorities
- Bounded rationality
- Time and energy limitation

Short-termism categories

- Cost cutting
- Reduction of working capital and cash investment
- (Selective) divestiture

Strategic delay

- Reduced corporate activity (e.g. Merger & Acquisitions)
- Procrastination of strategic activity (inertia)

FIGURE 2.1 Determinants and effects of short-termism

decipher and act upon other more strategic, longer-term plans. If more time or energy is not invested in the decision-making process, decisions will take longer and be untimely or involve less than enough analysis, thus running the risk of being inaccurate. Given a board's limitations on time and energy during crisis, it focuses on the short term; this inevitably brings with it the opportunity cost of delaying other less urgent but still important concerns. This is often at a significant (though hard to quantify) cost, one that relates to future impact on results such as losses of opportunity, eroded competitive position or competitive advantage. So, short-termism provides a further interpretative key: decisions that take longer to make and are less accurate are among the outcomes of boards' decision-making under crisis. We will come back to this point with empirical evidence from our interviews in Chapter 3.

Short-term focus at the board of directors' level is revealed by increased deliberate focus in the following actions: (a) cost reduction, (b) working capital and cash investments reduction, (c) selective divestiture and (d) at times divestiture of critical assets. In Chapter 3 we shall report that, according to our interviewees' accounts, the intensity of crisis felt in the boardroom will directly lead to an increased relevance and frequency of the tactical moves above. But problems tend to come in pairs. Increased boardroom short-term oriented focus is often coupled with reduced strategic activity on all fronts. A preference for short-term performance may lead to unintended consequences for the long-term value-adding capability of the firm (Marginson and McAulay, 2008).

Boards' short-termism mainly depends upon a conscious choice to focus on the most immediate issues. However, it may be also an outcome of the difficulty for boards to *make ends meet*, so they inadvertently concentrate on the short term. One of our interviewees for this book confessed: 'I'd go even further than [talking about] selective divestiture. Even if the board's intention [when divesting] is often selective divestiture, it is not always the case and sometimes the reaction is just divesting— not necessarily selectively, but *critical assets*—we strengthen the cash position now, thinking we will solve this later (e.g. recover this asset or a similar one)' (emphasis added).

Inevitably, and particularly during crisis, survival puts a very strong short-term pressure on dominant stockholders (i.e. for non-listed firms)—or the tyranny of the stock market in the case of listed organizations (Dobbin and Jung, 2010). In such conditions, boards appear to simply choose between two evils: long-term risk for the organization or short-term threat for survival.

Based on what we have said so far, we can more generally envisage that intensified crisis in the boardroom will be directly related to a reduced volume of corporate activity. Our interviewees seem to suggest the idea that the selection process of corporate activity opportunities is more careful during crisis. This is something yet to be tested as the crisis is not yet over. However, qualitative evidence seems to go in that direction. We purport, in sum, that crisis intensity in the boardroom may be directly related to value-creating effectiveness of corporate activity. Of course, there might be countervailing arguments; for example, funding can be (much) more difficult to access and this fact can be causal to reduced corporate activity, as well as that prices tend to be cheaper during crisis, fostering the chance of better deals.

Given the complexities and turbulence of the environment during crisis, boards of directors are expected to behave in a more diligent fashion regarding investments, forced to optimize the use of corporate funds by increased scarcity of resources. Crisis becomes, then, a natural experiment for boards of directors in relation to the efficiency of corporate activity. If this proved true, it would paradoxically reveal that reducing freedom of choice for boards with abundant resources—and often without enough satisfactory investment opportunities—or using control mechanisms to prevent this type of empire-building behavior, might promote a better use of corporate resources and benefit all stakeholders, an argument related to the traditional conceptualization on agency costs of free cash flow (Jensen, 1986).

Across our research we have seen—even within the same industry—very different time orientations (short-term versus long-term focus) in decision-making. We found companies within the same industry reacting in radically different ways: some behave in a more short-termist fashion during crisis, while others think about the long run even more visibly than during expansion. Among the viable explanations for this kind of differences in behaviors, one mentioned by several interviewees is ownership structure. Companies with a block-holding participation seem to promote a different time focus—usually longer term oriented—of decision-making under crisis.

The effect of ownership structure on strategy has been argued before in strategic management literature, albeit with conflicting results. Shareholder myopia might be behind executive short-termism (Samuel, 2000; 2001) and a large ownership proportion tends to reduce pressures for sacrificing long-term growth for short-term profit. Then, in principle, block-holder participation in ownership should negatively mediate the relationship between crisis intensity at the boardroom and short-termism. However, at the same time, block-holders or proprietary directors (those representing owners) may act against the long-term interest of the focal firm to protect their own short-term self-interest, for instance the value of their investment, the risk of dilution or reduced political power, to name just a few. This opportunistic behavior—self-interest with guile (Williamson, 1985)—would provide some support to the argument that block-holder participation in ownership would then mediate in the positive direction the relationship between crisis intensity in the boardroom and short-termism.

No doubt, the percentage of control is relevant for ownership, but stability also is. Besides the block-holding participation degree, another factor affecting the intensity of short-termism is the stability of this participation. It has been suggested (Edmans, 2009; Bushee, 1998) that the orientation to protect the longer term against the short term will be particularly prominent when the participation is stable in time. Thus, those stockholders with a long tenure as stockholders and a dominant participation will not be so tempted to act in a short-termist way during crisis.

In sum, the odds are that dominant and stable stockholders will be less prone to be short-sighted as a result of the crisis. The size and stability of the owners' stake influence their posture towards the business, relying more dependably on the long-term performance of the business rather than on short-term results.

Centralization and intensity of crisis

As we discuss in more depth in Chapter 4, increased centralization seems to be a likely outcome of crisis in the boardroom. This is consistent with previous literature on the topic (Gladstein and Reilly, 1985; Pfeffer, 1978; Hermann, 1963; Smart and Vertinsky, 1977; Staw, Sandelands and Dutton, 1981). Figure 2.2 reports the main determinants and consequences of centralization of decision-making.

At the organizational level, a key underlying factor explaining this centralization tendency is board risk aversion. Risk aversion has been widely used in management and finance literatures, but it has been comparatively less covered in experimental research and its modeling is scantier (Holt and Laury, 2002). Risk aversion increases during crisis, both at the individual and boardroom levels. On the one hand, this increase in boardroom risk aversion may be a reaction to reduce the degree of environmental equivocality for the organization (Weick, 1969) or a simply self-interested, opportunistic reaction (Williamson, 1975; 1985).

Our field evidence more realistically supports opportunism, as crisis bears more individual risks and legal and reputational liabilities for each board member (and for the board as a whole) and, therefore, it can be expected that tendency to self-interest is intensified during crisis.

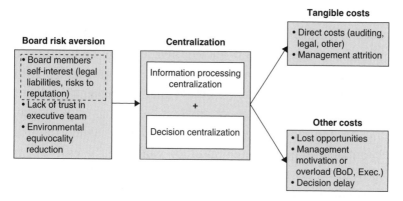

FIGURE 2.2 Suggested determinants and consequences of centralization during crisis

If we admit the former, a higher board risk aversion would be expected when crisis is deeper, in other words, when it is more intensively perceived by the board of directors. However, it might be possible that the positive relationship among risk aversion and crisis intensity changes during very intense crisis (as in 'life or death' situations) and promotes risk-seeking behaviors. At the same time, the way a specific decision or choice is framed may promote risk-seeking behaviors instead of risk-averse ones (Tversky and Kahneman, 1986). In sum, 'normal' risk levels may promote risk avoidance, and 'above normal' risk (much more common during periods of deep crisis) may eventually promote risk-seeking behaviors. As a consequence, board risk aversion might follow an inverted 'U shape' relationship with crisis intensity as perceived in the boardroom.

Centralization under crisis has two main faces: an increased demand of reporting information by the board and a stronger constriction in control about the actual decision to be taken. These two faces correspond to the concepts of: (a) centralized information processing, and (b) centralized decision-making.

The increasingly centralized information processing is seen in the need of the boardroom to satisfy a more in-depth understanding of corporate issues. Board risk aversion seems to be behind this centralization of information processing in its relationship with crisis intensity. Therefore, we believe that the higher the board's risk aversion, the larger information-processing centralization will be. The most extreme outcome of this inclination towards information-processing centralization would be the well-known idea of 'analysis paralysis', also an augmented risk in the boardroom during crisis.

Centralization has been widely presented in management literature as the authority to make decisions affecting the organization (Pugh *et al.*, 1963). It conveys an increased constriction in control and a more centralized process of decision-making. More decision-making is done in the boardroom during crisis: first, because decisions during crisis tend to be more complex (in other words, decisions entailing an increased level of risk); second, because managers reporting to senior officers will often be prone to 'delegate' upwards in order to reduce risks for them personally. Previous management literature is consistent with this increase in centralization of decision-making during crisis (Pfeffer, 1981). Given the curvilinear relationship already suggested between board risk aversion and crisis intensity, centralization in decision-making will be higher when the board's risk aversion is higher.

One of the driving forces of this process of centralization in the boardroom is the role that the CEO (or chairperson, when (s)he is also executive) plays in the decision-making process, and to which extent (s)he exerts control over the rest of the board. CEO dominance has been studied for a long time now (Finkelstein, 1992; Haleblian and Finkelstein, 1993) and helps us to shape the effect of formal power on decision-making centralization during crisis. It can be expected that during crisis, due to crisis-induced uncertainty, CEO risk aversion will grow and a more powerful CEO (in other words, a dominant CEO) will apply his/her power in order to increase centralization on decision-making, not just using the opportunity to get more power, but *because* of this increased risk aversion and his/her ability to exert formal power.

In other words, CEO dominance will act as a *moderator* of the relationship between crisis intensity and degree of centralization. From a practical standpoint, this means that pre-existing traits of power among the board are likely to lead to a more intense degree of centralization, in both dimensions of information processing and centralization of decision.

A particular case of CEO dominance is duality (when the CEO and the chairperson is the same person). Duality is also an objective indicator of formal power (Finkelstein, 1992; Haleblian and Finkelstein, 1993) and, thus, duality will similarly ease their use of power under crisis (Zajac and Westphal, 1996; Jensen and Zajac, 2004). When there is a dual CEO, the degree of centralization will be higher *even* with the same level of perceived intensity of crisis. It has long been argued—and is recommended in many corporate governance codes of good practice (e.g. FRC, 2010)—that a formal separation between the role of the chairperson and the role of the CEO is beneficial to keep a balanced quality of government at the top. This is particularly relevant during crisis in order to prevent an excessive usage of power by the CEO: checks and balances now become more important than before.

Formalization, as the tendency to provide formal procedures to follow, has long been known as an organizational tactic to increase coordination and control (Hage and Aiken, 1966), as well as a means to protect property rights or to avoid risks of moral hazard (Foss and Foss, 2005; Gulati and Singh, 1998). This is often the case during crisis. In fact, formalization is often promoted by directors in light of growing risk of liabilities. They more usually intensify control of decision during crisis by enhancing formalization of decision process in the boardroom under the form of a more formal scheduling of agenda, ratification of choices via voting of decisions and more formalized minutes.

A comparable strategy is also used during crisis by the chairpersons/CEOs (e.g. via formalization of reporting) with similar motives, in order to more effectively control decision outcome and to *infuse* the decision-making process across the board with formalities (i.e. to share accountability). In principle, when crisis is higher, and boards perceive it as such, the degree of formalization in decision-making will be higher. Although no formal minutes will keep a directorate safe in case of serious failure or malpractice, this is a most common strategy that (according to our interviewees) directorates use in order to shield themselves from increased risk.

Centralization is, after all, the concentration of decision-making in the upper levels of organizational hierarchy (Child, 1972; Marsh, 1992; Carter and Cullen, 1984) and this is what has happened on many boards during crisis. Besides formalization, intermediate structures or decision levels (e.g. delegated executive committees) are de facto eliminated (or put aside) in order to enforce centralization of decision-making processes. An example for this centralization trend could be the reduction of size in these intermediate structures in the decision-making process or the hierarchical *delayering* of these (or other) decision structures when decision-making capacity has been centralized elsewhere (for instance, in a more reduced subgroup of the board team).

Another example is the amplification in control of these groups (in other words, drilling down more deeply or in more topics).

In a way, the risk aversion felt in the boardroom has grown with the intensity of crisis, then the size of the key decision-making team (e.g. the executive committee) has been reduced accordingly in order to concentrate their influence (even eliminating or putting traditional structures aside to have the board *directly* controlling the management effort): more power concentrated in the hands of less people in order to 'control' the perceived increased risk of liabilities for the directorate.

The paradox of this behavior, as we shall explain in Chapter 4, is that this centralization has implications both in terms of costs or delay (e.g. bottlenecks) and executive motivation. Increased demotivation of executives, due to the loss of control in the decision-making process (as in increased micro-management from the board), has been (and still is) a common and perverse side effect of board behavior. For this reason, in the following pages we will analyze the implications of CEO/chairperson or owners' decision-making centralization on the motivation of independent directors and executive directors during crisis.

We suggest that hubris and overconfidence bias may influence centralizing behaviors (Kahneman, Slovic and Tversky, 1982) as well as motivation. The concept of hubris describes an extreme pride or arrogance. This idea refers to an exaggerated confidence about one's own judgment that may diverge from 'objective' standards (Hayward and Hambrick, 1997; Hayward, Shepherd and Griffin, 2006; Hiller and Hambrick, 2005). Our interviewees suggest that this hubris (on the side of the chairperson/CEO and/or the owners/proprietary directors) may influence the motivation of executive and independent directors. Based on this, it can be argued that hubristic behaviors contribute to tension in the boardroom during crisis.

In fact, we contend that hubris rather than CEO dominance or power (Finkelstein, 1992; Haleblian and Finkelstein, 1993) or block-holding participation is the factor that most influences motivation of independent directors and executive directors. Both CEO dominance or dominant shareholder participation are objective power indicators and, in principle, could be known *a priori*, previous to board enrollment by executive or independent directors; while experiencing hubris requires working contact familiarity with hubristic actors in the boardroom (chairperson/ CEOs or block-holding proprietary directors).

Based on this, we argue that a relationship between hubristic CEO/chairperson behavior and motivation of the directorate holds particularly strong during crisis. The relationship between these hubristic behaviors and motivation (in the rest of the top team) is deemed to be negative; the motivation of executive directors (and even that of independent directors) will be negatively related to these hubristic behaviors. If motivation is an antecedent of attrition, we can conclude that hubristic CEOs or chairpersons will see, during crisis (and also very likely during expansion), an increased number of (undesired) departures from the board among other directors. We expect a similar dynamic for proprietary directors or owners, or block-holding proprietary directors. When owners demonstrate more hubristic behaviors in the boardroom, the odds for executive directors' and independent directors exit will be higher.

The overall lesson for senior leaders (CEOs, chairpersons, owners) is that during crisis they need to be particularly sensitive of their own behaviors, because they might inadvertently contribute to increased tension and decreased team effectiveness.

While all these courses of action may help directors or CEOs to reduce perceived ambiguity and risk, we believe that this bureaucracy-oriented behavior (that is, oriented to reduce variance in organizational behaviors) might impact quality, cost and timeliness of decision-making. In formulating our rationale for short-termism and centralization of boardroom decision-making under crisis, we need also to explore the expectations and implications about the micro-dynamics of boardroom decision-making during crisis, apparently characterized by increased parochialism and conflict.

Parochialism and conflict in boardrooms during crisis

Self-interest is intensified under crisis, an observation already present in previous literature (Weick, 1993). Reduced slack under crisis intensifies incompatibility of priorities and conflict among objectives, increasing parochialism at the board level. This parochialism leads to a more complex balance of interests, inducing increased risk for decision quality and timeliness. Parochialism is accentuated even more, given the substantively more complex nature of boardroom discussions and due to the increased intensity of debate while in crisis. Both factors contribute to escalated conflict and tension in the decision-making process under crisis and end up in a more uncertain balance for decision-making quality and timeliness in the boardroom (Mishra, 1996; Hermann, 1963; Turner, 1976).

Our interviews reveal, as will be reported in Chapter 5, that even in the *organized hierarchy* of the boardroom there are several features of the organized anarchies as described by Cohen, March and Olsen (1972) with their 'garbage-can' model of choice. It has to be mentioned, though, that the boardroom is not unanimously (internally) seen as a purely hierarchical setting. In the words of one of our interviewees: 'The CEO may be the king/queen with his/ her executive team but within the board (s)he is only one more; not necessarily the only one, or even obviously an important one.' The former chairman of a large company mentions: 'This [exertion of hierarchical power] depends on the focal leader [chairperson/ CEO]. Some people [chairpersons/CEOs] promote discussion and admit push backs, some others do not.'

Arguably, conflicting self-interests seem to be motives behind this parochialism (Williamson, 1975). This combination of increased complexity of problem-solving, confronted goals and increased tension leads frequently to a delay in decision. Even when there is no decision-making delay, parochialism and conflicting interests push in the direction of a decreased quality of decision. In other words, the decision may be taken early (e.g. through the influence of one or more groups or individuals in the boardroom or by the pressing urgency of executives) and be ineffective, indeed solving no problem (decision by *oversight*: Cohen, March and Olsen, 1972). This model of choice is even more likely under crisis in which the executive team presses hard the board of directors to take faster decisions.

From the perspective of the decision-making process, our research seems to show that pressures from crisis will affect both *access structures* (mapping of issues onto choices) as well as *decision structures* (mapping of decision makers onto choices). Indeed, crisis increases the number of issues for the same or less choices, strengthening the stream of problems. At the same time, crisis affects the decision structure: energy from decision makers is likely to be decreased (due to the increased stream of issues) while choices are stable or reduced. The outcome, as observed through our interviews, could be that less effective problem-solving happens during crisis. Moreover, when the crisis is particularly intense, the ineffective problem-solving process could lead to decreased executive motivation (the exploration of personal motivation and job satisfaction issues are, however, well beyond the scope of this book).

A competing tension with the procrastinating board dynamics inferred from the former discussion is the pressure of executives encouraging urgency of decision from the boardroom. This pressure of executives towards the board to take a decision is based on issue urgency (Julian and Ofori-Dankwa, 2008; Dutton, Stumpf and Wagner, 1990). Executives press hard to have the boardroom make (or legitimate) decisions, because actual organizational performance may be contingent on effective decision-making (that is, timeliness is part of the nature of effective decisions).

This pressure from managers may, however, have uncertain effects on the final outcome in the decision-making process. Due to the longer analysis process for decision-making during crisis, when executives are able to effectively press or persuade the board to take a quicker decision, this will be often at the cost of less or incomplete decision analysis or increased board workload. We contend, finally, that this executive urgency will be a moderating variable between crisis intensity and decision timing. This seems to suggest that crisis intensity at board level will be directly related to less effective problem-solving; the more intense the crisis, the less effective the decision-making process. In Chapters 3 to 5 we will describe in more detail how these skeptical arguments are suggested by our interviewees.

chapter 3

Short-Termism: What You Can Do Tomorrow Will Largely Depend on Your Thinking Today

Focus on the short term has been suggested to be causal to the crisis situations during the first part of the 21st century and, specifically, causal to the one we are currently experiencing (Davies, 2010). For example, Dobbin and Jung (2010) suggested that the domination of 'the quarter'—the quarterly profit report and its accuracy with analysts' forecasts and projections—had already become the center of CEO focus and attention in the early 1990s. This pressure has lately increased due to amplified uncertainty under crisis, which in turn creates stronger incentives to focus on quarterly results. In this chapter, we unfold the concept of short-termism during crisis and discuss how it affects boards' decision-making.

Why short-termism?

Quarterly results present an interesting paradox: although a milestone through which to measure business performance, they turn out to be the objective of business performance rather than the means of measuring it. Besides the potential risk of this force for the 'true and fair view' of financial statements, our interviewees report that this pressure for the short term might threaten sustainability. Stewardship may not be perceived as important as short-term results and, hence, the risk of postponing important decisions increases for the sake of shorter-term results. This is not to say that short term always offsets long-term interest (on the contrary: there is very often no long term without short term) but it is an additional force stretching management or, at least, influencing business performance communication (to external stakeholders).

This drift may be intensified by certain compensation tools, particularly when they intensely reward short-term results. Dobbin and Jung (2010) suggest that external pressures together with some executive compensation instruments (e.g. stock options) created an incentive for earnings management, a well-known practice of using discretion in financial reporting in order to inflate earnings and potentially exceed market expectations, either in the present or in the future (Martin, 2011; Healy and Wahlen, 1999).[1]

A former executive director, knowledgeable in the corporate governance field, states in relation to dominant compensation schemes: 'There is no way corporate governance can do any better if (when) there are not at all consequences for mistakes. Large compensation packages (have been paid) with no

---

[1] Note that we are not talking here about fraud or manipulation, but about those gray areas where accounting rules and criteria for expense accounting and revenue recognition may establish a difference in results. While discretion about accounting (for instance, selecting the most convenient way for the company to reflect any operation, *within* US GAAP or other applicable criteria) is correct, acceptable and often used when feasible in the best company interest, this practice may veer off and potentially be something else. Indeed, one of the intentions of Sarbanes-Oxley Act (2002) was to prevent such type of risks.

possibility of any corporate restitution in case something goes wrong (later); this does not indeed encourage wise decision-making (just the opposite seems truer).'

These dynamics may be exacerbated by external crisis or economic adversity. During crisis, management runs the risk of postponing other more strategic (and thus more important, despite less urgent) concerns by concentrating only on shorter-term concerns. Deciding about future directions is, not surprisingly, more difficult during crisis, given crisis-idiosyncratic increased uncertainty. For example, the evolution of the mergers and acquisitions (M&A) marketplace, whose activity plummeted at the beginning of the current financial crisis period and is yet below its pre-crisis level,[2] is an enlightening indicator of this procrastinating strategy (see Figure 3.1, extracted from *New York Times* (2011) citing Thomson Reuters data). Crisis reduces (or, more properly, this crisis has reduced) the volume of this kind of strategic move. Of this volume (as at the end of 2010) one-third approximately was the US share of this market (*New York Times*, 2011).

However, this intensity of strategic activity is not necessarily a proxy for corporate success. This is something to be analyzed more carefully in light of evidence about value destruction in large corporate transactions, particularly company acquisitions (Haleblian *et al.*, 2009). It had been previously argued (Jensen, 1986) that under specific circumstances (e.g. large cash flows in excess of high-return investment opportunities) reduced corporate activity may be beneficial in order to avoid empire-building on the part of executive managers. If that proved correct, this crisis

---

[2] In fact, the worldwide volume of corporate activity only began to rise in 2010, but still far off the peak in 2007. More recently (2012) the estimation of the volume of this market is still in US$ 2.25 trillion (EY website, Dec. 2012) still very far from the 2007 peak.

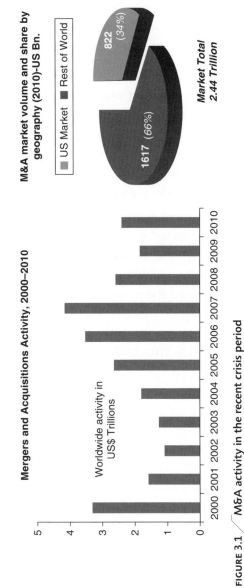

FIGURE 3.1 M&A activity in the recent crisis period

Source: New York Times, Jan 2011.

has avoided many value destruction initiatives (through reduced corporate activity) but, at the same time, this reduced volume of corporate activity has been in many ways a thermometer for economic (in)activity; important decisions, particularly those more strategic in nature, have been postponed.

Postponing those more strategic issues imposes other opportunity costs and may lead to losing competitive position. In the words of an executive director in a private equity firm: 'The issue is that you may be postponing strategic decisions and this pushes the business to a dead end.' Another interviewee, the chairman of a service company, acknowledges this risk and summarizes this concern in the following way: 'I believe that, indeed, the ones who are going to survive and emerge better prepared from this crisis are those who take opportunities and assume more risks, looking into the longer term. You cannot just look at the figures. Qualitative issues are very important; you need to look beyond the numbers.'

How common is short-termism during crisis?

A significant paradox is that despite the notion that short-termism might have been partially behind the inception of crisis (Davies, 2010) there is little question that, besides reduced corporate activity, increased short-termism is still one of the preferred reactions of boardrooms under crisis. Concentrating on the short term to prepare later strategic moves is a classical sequence. A former CEO, now independent director in several companies, describes it this way:

> This has stages. In a first stage, you have to 'stop the beat', have risks under control at a reduced cost. This is managing a

'war economy'. Once this is done, in a second stage you have to diversify, see how to increase income, how to milk the cow further, or buy new cows (or goats). However, I have to admit that this crisis is very long and this initial 'cost freezing' phase is getting longer and displacing the second.

An executive director defines this same behavior clearly and succinctly: 'I have to work more than ever and, therefore, we have to give things up. We concentrate on the shorter-term issues and postpone those more strategic in nature. It is both a conscious but inevitable choice, because we have to make ends meet.' He continues: 'Strategic plans are revised every month.'

This deferral of strategic decision-making is frequently intensified if the firm has not previously developed a substantial internal discipline for strategy-making. For instance, companies without a formal strategy process in place—those in which the strategy process is too dependent on individual initiatives or isolated actors, rather than on an orchestrated and planned managerial effort—seem to procrastinate more clearly about strategic decision-making. The CEO of a multibillion global company acknowledges this risk: 'It is very difficult to plan when all around you is falling; you lose the ground under your feet and begin to be unsure about everything … Now it is crucial to have a serious strategy development process in place. Starting from scratch, from a blank piece of paper in such a situation is the litmus test to see if you are a good or bad strategist as a CEO.'

This is also aggravated because there is often a lack of valuable input from the most immediate environment. In fact, informational input to make good strategic choices, such as external sources of inspiration coming from interaction with outward actors (as in clients, suppliers, bankers, advisors, and the like), is often missed. Opportunities may appear less often and be less clear. The CEO above explains this the following way: 'When things go well out there, we have a zillion consultants and investment bankers queuing at the door to sell us ideas about new businesses to be pursued here or there. This doesn't happen anymore now. Now there are less deals and these guys have quit or have been fired. The difficult thing about strategizing during crisis is often facing a blank sheet of paper, with less (or little) external inspiration.'

Consistent with most organizational theory developed in the 1970s, which suggests the impact of the environment on firms' performance and survival (Meyer and Rowan, 1977; Hannan and Freeman, 1977), the intensity of the crisis is heavily conditioned by the industry in which a company competes, usually even more than the characteristics of the individual (focal) organization. This is, after all, a key trait of a systemic crisis. For instance, the current crisis does not seem to have affected companies in countercyclical or high-innovation rate industries such as luxury goods, computer technology (cloud computing, computing security and storage) and energy (*Forbes*, 2008; *The Atlantic*, 2011). Yet most mature industries have been strongly damaged, unless companies show attention to long-term goals and emerging markets are effectively targeted. An independent director in a very mature industry, asserts: 'We have just had the most successful quarter of our history and our previous benchmark was the former quarter: in fact this crisis was an opportunity for us to explore other (international emerging) markets.' He continues: 'I am not sure that strategic issues have been postponed; not in our case. I have seen significant plans of investment in the company I am a director with. But to be honest, we have not been seriously affected by crisis; the local market is really tiny as a percentage of total revenues and our main markets were in developing countries and hence growing. [There is] no hysteria of not having enough cash in the bank to afford the next month's payroll.'

Another exception to this short-term orientation pattern might have been when companies had a dominant stockholder more prone to assume risks. An independent director in a technology company describes an example of this situation: 'We are (now) working a lot on the strategic level. Having a chairman like ours (who is also a dominant stockholder) may influence us not to forget strategy during crisis. In fact, we have recently launched a new strategic plan.'

Aside from these exceptions, the majority of our interviewees reported that during crisis their companies have been (and still are) in a time of increased short-term orientation. Those interviewed (executive directors, chairpersons/CEOs and independent/non-executive directors) report almost unanimously that the largest part of boardroom action during crisis has been focused around short-term-oriented actions, often centered on the protection of the cash position in the balance sheet.

The chairman of a large company stresses this idea, describing the dominant mindset of many boards: 'Boards reduce their level of ambition under crisis; this is what I have most seen. They pursue more modest goals, things anchored on the most immediate issues, rather than longer time prospects and more strategic bets.' An independent director with substantial experience in the service industry states: 'Mostly any type of asset might have gone through a (sometimes deep) depreciation process these days. The only exception is cash, because while in a deflationary situation in which most assets lose value, cash increases relatively its own, and it is liquid.' Not surprisingly, and as we will see, most organizational reactions have tended to reduce as much as possible cash consumption via investments or outflows (delaying investments when feasible or via cost reduction) or to stockpile cash when possible such as, for example, selling underutilized assets.

Based on the field data and for the sake of clarity, we have grouped short-term-oriented reactions to crisis into four main operational categories: (a) cost-cutting (reduction of selling, general and administrative expenditures and reduction of headcount structure in all areas); (b) working capital and cash investment reductions; (c) selective divestiture (as in sale of underperforming or non-strategic assets, when possible, in order to cash in). In addition to these short-term-oriented reactions, there are other more purely short-termist reactions, such as: (d) divesting critical (core) assets in the face of crisis. Such categories are presented in Table 3.1.

TABLE 3.1   Board short-termist strategies during crisis

Main category of short-termism	Examples
(1) Cost reduction	• Cost reduction programs (energy, general and overhead expenses) • Layoff or restructuring programs • Internalization of (previously outsourced) activities to leverage remaining internal excess capacity (reducing external variable costs and potential—internal—severance costs)
(2) Working capital and cash investment reductions	• New credit conditions (both for clients and suppliers) • Paralysis or delay in purchases and investments • Cash payout reductions (e.g. dividends are reduced or stock dividends are used instead of cash dividends) • Transformation of long-term liabilities into equity (e.g. to reduce non-discretionary cash outflows)
(3) Selective divestiture	• Sale of non-critical asset • Sale of non-core participation or subsidiary ownership
(4) Divestiture of critical asset	• Sale of critical or strategic asset • Sale of key participation or subsidiary ownership

Cost-reduction exercises

Cost-cutting is often the first natural reaction under crisis, particularly when there is a shortage in demand. An independent director of a large company with operations in many areas of the world puts it quite simply: 'If revenues fall, we have to reduce costs.' As blunt as this may seem, it implies that often during crisis the most immediate move is not trying to compensate for loss of income in traditional business (such as looking for additional opportunities) but reducing by some fraction the total amount of costs. The dominant mindset is not offsetting crisis via increased revenue, but through cost-freezing. The rationale is strong, because cost-cutting activities usually have more foreseeable results, at least in the shorter term, while revenue-generation initiatives bring typically more unclear outcomes.

Another interviewee, an independent director with a long tenure as an executive across several industries, agrees that cost-cutting is probably the most immediate reaction: 'The first step in a crisis is always trying to "take shelter" and have risks under control at a reduced cost.' Another independent director theorizes about this reaction and says: 'Cost-cutting is always the immediate reaction under crisis and this has been enough to survive during most of previous crises; but it is not working for this one. Using a war metaphor, previous crises were conventional wars but this is a new, non-conventional war, and thus we need innovative strategies and new weapons to fight this one.'

An independent director of several listed and private companies reflects about the nature of these boardroom reactions: 'During crisis, all changes in the boardroom. It is not any more business development and sales executives who present stuff to the board, but now it is the turn for folks in finance, for the auditing people, for those in (management) control functions and others—all those trying to manage risks.'

Interestingly, organizations try to maintain headcount structure as much as they can during crisis. This has been shown in countries such as Spain and Belgium, who have among the most rigid labor regulations in developed economies worldwide (Pissarides, 2011). Most likely this happens due to the high severance costs in these countries. The public and social cost of the currently high unemployment rate and the importance of talent in their businesses are often secondary concerns. An executive chairman serving in a company with global operations asserts: 'We made a conscious effort to control headcount, not firing people if possible, but through frozen hiring and vegetative exits.'

From a cost perspective, reducing headcount structure is often the last resource: boards authorize this move generally only when there is no other evident remedy for survival. Another chairman in the technology industry reports: 'We began to suffer late in 2010 and I had to reduce headcount (even if this was not what I wanted), because of the importance (and cost); some key personnel had to leave.' The strategy of engaging in close (and continuous) conversation with the boardroom is, as will be discussed later, one of the preferred approaches of CEOs during crisis to reduce their individual exposure to errors: they meticulously involve the rest of the boardroom in the overall process of decision-making, so that none can later allege ignorance (we return to this topic in more detail in Chapter 5).

Reducing working capital and protecting cash

The second short-term-oriented category of decision-making is minimizing working capital investments and cash out-flows. This is a logical corollary of the consideration of cash as a major value to be protected during crisis.

An executive director in a large firm comments: 'Plenty of the decisions these days for many companies are about survival, so we think we will care about this and that (important things) later, but now we have to save ourselves.' He continues: 'Concentrating on the short term is protecting the cash position, which is particularly important now, with a more limited funding situation.'

An independent director in a mature industry also mentions working capital management as a predominant short-term focus under crisis: 'Reducing costs, often by using multiple competitive bidding (thus, reducing prices). And then crushing them [suppliers] with payment conditions.' Indeed, due to crisis—and accentuated by more limited access to funding—the pressure of large companies towards their suppliers is particularly strong. To put it simply, firms buy less (or postpone purchase) and stock less when feasible, because demand is weaker; and they do as much as possible to collect soon and pay later, reducing operating needs of funding and creating a more comfortable cash position. Obviously, this management behavior might have a perverse impact on the rest of the environment—not only suppliers, but also clients.

Cash is preserved when possible. This apparent obsession with reducing working capital investment and protecting cash may end up resulting in bad or too myopic management decisions, for instance dropping (potentially) attractive investment opportunities. The CEO in a global company reports something similar: 'We have to protect cash, we have to protect cash. That is the mantra. Consuming cash is badly perceived by the [stock] market and is later penalized. That's the dominant thinking among the board and drove us to discard some really good opportunities.' The same idea is supported by the chairman of a large financial institution: 'We had several hundred millions in cash, but we were not initially allowed to invest in Y acquisition opportunity.'

The paradox is that good opportunities might be lost, even if—as is often argued by our interviewees—opportunities frequently remain up for grabs for longer periods of time. This occurs in part because there are expectations of price improvement for both sides in the transaction (that is, lower for the prospective buyer, and higher for the prospective seller, often in need of funding), which is partially due to decision-making processes during crisis becoming longer and less effective for both buyers and sellers.

Selective divestiture

The third short-term-oriented category of action is selective divestiture. Asset-funding was less demanding in the recent past with abundant and inexpensive money. The situation is now different with a shortage in credit in several countries (Banco de España, 2011). An independent director in the R&D-intensive business puts it this way: 'Which decisions do we take faster now? Those related to survival and divestiture.' At the same time, a CEO in a multibillion company confesses: 'During this crisis, we have decided on selective divestiture (in some activities/ countries); particularly in those where we had less experience or country knowledge.'

This is also the case mentioned by an independent director in a large business with operations in several continents: 'It is about reducing non-core assets, not core assets, all of it related to [financial] leverage. For instance, certain activity with very specific assets in [the country] where we knew we could sell, we had an idea of what the price to obtain could be, and we thought that this [asset] was not critical for the business in that geographical area. Thus, we sold.'

Often these divestiture decisions have been suboptimal because, as mentioned earlier, the market expectations for price have changed. Prices fall. The market is then more reluctant to accept the price premium that many businesses had during the previous expansion period (when their assets were bought or brought up). Thus, paradoxically, the intention of maximizing the use of financial resources ends up creating additional write-offs in their profit and loss statements, particularly when these divestiture decisions are related to real estate or other physical assets, but also in the case of participation in companies and businesses.

Selling the family jewels

From time to time, boards decide to sell critical assets; that is, those crucial for their future business performance, sometimes at a huge discount or, at least, lower than what they were valued at during the peak periods. This is the most purely short-termist action, because it involves a preference for short-term performance driving undesired implications for the long-term value-adding capabilities of the firm (Marginson and McAulay, 2008). Often, such decisions during crisis might have been related to the shrinking access to credit or to the pressure for short-term performance induced by capital markets (e.g. delivering quarterly results according to industry or analysts' expectations or aligned to previous company communications about results). The chief executive of a large business explains this perverse logic, talking about divestiture of critical assets: 'It is not only that we save what we can, or divest what we do not consider critical; it is often much worse: sometimes critical assets are sold, thinking (naively) that we will find a similar replacement later.' This has been the case for many companies during crisis, particularly in capital-intensive industries, often trapped by financial constraints and under high pressure to deleverage or reduce their financial burdens (especially for those that expanded gently during the previous upturn). The paradox has been (and still is) that in order to face their financial commitments they need to sell at a discount the assets critical for their future, which they bought (or built) at a premium, often significantly more expensive than current (falling) market prices, thus putting their future at increased risk.

Beyond short-termism

These short-termist behaviors are not without clear drawbacks. As mentioned earlier, a crucial opportunity cost of this short-term focus is the deferral of key strategic decisions about growth or corporate activity, which may be a risk because of the potential loss of competitive position or strategic opportunity. At the same time, this short-term orientation often has other implications in terms of the quality and cost of the decision (e.g. additional internal effort or external help and associated cost— external advisors such as lawyers, bankers or consultants—to analyze information or input for decision-making).

The potential contradiction resulting from this analysis is that focusing primarily on the short run will not necessarily mean becoming any stronger after crisis. In fact, some contend that the converse is truer. An executive chairman in a large financial company illustrates this point: 'You need to behave like if you were in crisis during expansion (that's when problems are engendered) and in expansion mode under crisis, so as to take advantage of the opportunities that all crises offer. Otherwise, during crisis you can only try to survive.' He continues: 'The ones making fortunes now are going to be the ones that were more sober before (during the expansive period) and they will be able now to behave more aggressively.'

What our interviewees report reassures the idea that crisis may be accentuating short-termism. To be sure, most of the pressures that pushed management into short-term focus in the current pre-crisis situation (Dobbin and Jung, 2010) are still here—those external to firm factors (e.g. stock market pressure, the rating agencies and mass media, to name a few) and those internal to the firm (e.g. short-term-oriented compensation schemes, internal ownership structure, appetite for risk of block-holders). A possible interpretation is that crisis has intensified the sensitivity from all those forces towards short-term orientation.

Some other external, relatively new players such as proxy advisors (Choi, Fisch and Kahan, 2008) might have increasingly influenced boardroom behaviors during the current crisis, even if there is no clear evidence in the extant literature, or in our interviews, of a correlation between the intensity of crisis and proxy advisors' influence. Somehow, on the contrary, OECD (2010) suggested that proxy advisors should properly manage their conflicts of interest and compete in an open market. This would induce proxy advisors to avoid rigid positions over the corporate governance health of the companies whose shareholders they advise and, hence, 'release' pressure from some directorates.

We believe there are organizational and individual factors determining or explaining better this intensified short-termism during crisis (Laverty, 1996; Marginson and McAulay, 2008). Two main reasons for short-termism emerge with particular strength under crisis. The first is our bounded rationality (Simon, 1945, 1957), the formal way of evoking our limitations in cognition: human beings have cognitive limits, which under the increased uncertainty typical of crisis situations become central in conditioning board behaviors. This is seen as underpinning the idea of reduced slack in crisis or adverse environments (March, 1994). In decision-making we are always limited by our cognition and by the amount of time and energy we can devote to making decisions—for example, being aware of issues in the first place, scanning our environment to gather and process information to face those issues, generating options, then prioritizing and selecting among them—and crisis accentuates the effect of these discerning limits. Due to this inherent bounded rationality and partially because of causal ambiguity (Powell, Lovallo and Caringal, 2006) our inability to 'maximize' grows larger during crisis.

Second, the amount of time and energy devoted to decision-making by individuals in the boardroom is limited. This is more notable particularly for busy boards, such as those in which directors have many roles, or other directorate appointments competing for their time and attention. There is some evidence that busy boards may not be good monitors of executive performance (Fich and Shivdasani, 2006). This is a vital concern under crisis as it is likely that boards will be facing more decision workload: there are more numerous and more difficult decisions to take.

In the words of the chairman of a large service company: 'It is a reasonable assumption to think that there are more decisions to make under crisis.' The CEO of a global firm puts it in a perhaps more nuanced way: 'During crisis decisions are more difficult or at least more complex; the process is always tougher, often nasty.' And another interviewee, a former director, asserts: 'People tend to become more risk averse during crisis, but that may be even riskier: important decisions get postponed and you may end up crashing, because you didn't do what you had to do.'

During crisis, as has been shown, behaviors in the boardroom tend to be more short-termist, often at the cost of decreased quality of decision, higher costs (e.g. external advice) and increased strategic risks (i.e. postponing potentially crucial decisions). All this characterizes boardroom decision-making during crisis as less strategic and predominantly focused on purely tactical concerns. In the next chapter we analyze how the decisions are taken during crisis—and who makes them.

4

'We Will Need to Check That': Centralization and Control in the Boardroom during Crisis

Most of us tend to control all that happens in our surroundings; this is second nature for human beings (Conner, 1992). One may argue that this is exactly one of the reasons why we have been able to survive for so long across evolution in front of much larger, faster and stronger predators.

From a management viewpoint this urge for control is well known to organizational theorists, beginning with the seminal *The Practice of Management* by Peter Drucker (1954). This impulse accentuates during crisis when rules to interpret the context are suspended, changed (or unknown) and, hence, executives try to get rid of as much as possible of this increased uncertainty. This process happens at the individual level, but organizational helms try also to do the same in the face of shifting environments during crisis.

Organizational strategies to reduce uncertainty in decision-making and in relation to the external environment have been a leading research topic for the last few decades. It would be difficult to reconcile here this vast research effort and to pay the deserved attention to, among others, contingency theory and the several institutional approaches discussing extant strategies for uncertainty reduction. We simply assume (and we take full responsibility for this oversimplification) that centralization and control of decision-making processes are considered as feasible strategies for uncertainty reduction by almost all organizational scholars taking part in the academic debate on this topic.

As a consequence, we focus our attention here on centralization and process control, arguing with Pfeffer (1978) that increased centralization and control are likely organizational outcomes of crisis and organizational threats. We therefore expect an increased focus on control among the board of directors during crisis. In such a situation, our interviews reveal that all the different characters on the board—the chairperson and/ or CEO, the owners (or proprietary directors on their behalf) and independent/non-executive directors—are significantly concerned about how to find a way to reduce the odds of errors. Centralization and process control seem to be dealt with as the quickest solutions. This occurs in spite of the differences in the actual boardroom influence of executive and independent directors across regions due to different governance practices or regulations, for example, Anglo-Saxon market practices versus dual governance structures in the German area. Interestingly, despite the globalization of codes of governance (Enrione, Mazza and Zerboni, 2006), country-based differences in governance practices are still present and resonate with the differences among the business systems (Whitley and Kristensen, 1997; Quack, Morgan and Whitley, 2000). Although beyond the scope of this volume, we hold that the question of resilience to crisis and globalization of governance structures and practices should deserve continued careful attention by academic research.

In this chapter we review in depth the main effects of centralization and control stemming from crisis (as it is perceived in the boardroom). Centralization takes several forms in operational processes and decision-making; we focus here on information-processing centralization and decision centralization. We then describe and discuss the strategies of centralization as reported by our interviewees. Finally, we outline the implications of decision-making centralization on boardroom life and operations.

Information-processing centralization

The urge for control often takes the shape of more information being demanded from the management team by the board and by other board committees such as auditing, nomination and remuneration. More reports are subsequently produced. This process is central to the concept of information-processing centralization (Gibbons, 2003).

According to one of our interviewees, a former CEO and now an independent director: 'More reviews are asked [by the board] from executives, more reviews, more revisions and plans, more about activities with losses or that could lose in the future, more reviews about things going well, making money (or not). A lot more review and questioning is done on all activities, *whether they are strategic or not*' (emphasis added). The chairman of a large European company suggests something similar: 'The depth of information [to be used in the decision-making process] is the same. But there is more variety in it. You ask for other issues. You ask it with higher frequency, things you'd normally see once a year, now you look at them two or three times [per year].'

This comment portrays a quite interesting dynamic within boards: the change in the selection of relevant information for decision-making. Board members do not just ask for deeper information on existing issues, but frequently ask for management information about new issues. This is consistent with the adoption of control practices to reduce uncertainty. Boards try to cope with crisis ambiguities by widening the range of matters under their direct supervision and by more frequently exerting access to managerial information. These are logical premises of centralization; boards may potentially have their voice over a wider set of topics, frequently operational, rather than solely strategic issues.

The executive chairman of a company in the corporate services domain makes the following comment: 'The board (particularly proprietary directors) demands more information and more options/scenarios of decision during crisis in order to gain an increased sense of control and to protect their investment.' This increased informational load, to a certain extent 'pollution', does not necessarily increase quality of decision. In fact, the converse could be true, as we will see later. In addition, there are other drawbacks such as misleading or contradictory information and the increased reporting struggle, as well as other implications such as decreased managerial motivation due to non-productive reporting time or to reduced attention (and time) devoted to effective management activities, to name just two important concerns. In addition, increased reporting may also involve the use of consultants or other advisors in order to legitimize interpretations of business reality. At the managerial level, reporting may become a key activity also to gain visibility and career opportunities; increased information demand at board level may produce *ad hoc* processes, new tasks, operations and ongoing bureaucratization at the organizational level. All this might have undesired implications in decision-making effectiveness (as in the cost or quality of the decision).

In plain terms, when the urge for control takes the shape of information-processing centralization, it often produces more effort for boardroom decision-making. It can be questioned if and when this effort leads to actual utility. Often more control leads to more attention and time devoted to the materiality of control, such as reports, analysis and meetings, rather than to substantive decision-making. Consequently (and paradoxically), increased control could lead to less control.

Centralization of decision processes

Centralization of information-processing goes hand in hand with a tighter constriction on control. This strongly affects executive motivation. Staw, Sandelands and Dutton (1981) claimed that under threat conditions, organizational control is increased, decisions of dominant members in the organization may prevail more readily, and the exercise of influence becomes more centralized. The decision-making power of managers is actually diminished during crisis as more (centralized) control results in decreased managerial discretion.

This centralization of authority in organizations under stress, and the increased dependence on leaders to take decisions, is seen as an adaptive response to external threat, because it places responsibility on those more vital to organizational values and goals (Staw, Sandelands and Dutton, 1981; Driskell and Salas, 1991) and to higher levels in the hierarchical structure (Hermann, 1963). Data from our field research suggest something very consistent with this scholarly analysis.

The former CEO in a large company, now an independent consultant, explains: 'During crisis everyone tries to increase control. Almost immediately, the CFO sees herself reporting to the Auditing (and Risks) Committee, the HR head is "kidnapped" by the Remuneration Committee and the CEO checks everything with the board. Both those up in the board and those below feel more comfortable.' We shall later return to this point, the intervention loop between board and senior management, because it might help explain the often risk-averse behavior happening on the board during crisis and its effect on managerial behaviors and motivation.

Both empirical evidence and existing literature on the topic takes us in the direction of centralization of influence as a key organizational reaction under threat or crisis (Gladstein and Reilly, 1985). There are two main natures in this increased centralization of decision. It might be: (a) centralization at board level (not only by the CEO, but by the board as such), and (b) CEO centralization within the board.

First, our fieldwork suggests that there is more centralization of decision at boardroom level. This centralizing attitude under crisis frequently implies more direct costs (such as increased cost of external consultants and advisors, auditors and legal counselors) in order to reduce uncertainty. Self-defending strategies, an alternative way of reducing personal risks, may be also an incentive to proceed this way (Mayer and Gavin, 2005).

The general manager of a large private company with board responsibilities in several other firms says: 'There is absolute terror (in the boardroom). It is an endless loop, a Kafkaesque spiral of cost. More costs (to have other opinions, to ensure and limit liabilities, etc.). It is a real snowball.' The CEO of a multibillion business provides specific examples of this behavior: 'There is a lot of worrying, e.g. on disclosure. For instance, we had to spend a lot of money on board-specific services. Crisis is a real business opportunity for wise external advisors.' An independent director in the financial services industry provides a fully coincident view: 'Executives (and the board) are requiring more analysis. Eventually, they end up asking for an external opinion (e.g. a consultant or lawyer) to contrast with executive opinion to have the board feel more comfortable.'

In theory, a more reflective and thought-out decision-making process, while it may be more costly, may be positive for decision quality, particularly when the situation is new and a different context and emerging variables are involved. However, this research suggests that there are also other undesirable outcomes offsetting this benefit. For example, deciding late may well be equivalent to deciding poorly. One of the worst of these downsides is the inevitable delay (or even abortion) of decision, particularly because decision-making speed is crucial in dynamic environments and crisis is practically the definition of a high-velocity environment (Bourgeois and Eisenhardt, 1988). This pattern (increasing the time and effort involved in taking a decision) does not always happen for the sake of decision quality; it may simply play a symbolic management role disguising own interest through stratagems (Westphal and Zajac, 1994; Zajac and Westphal, 1995).

The CEO in a global firm provides a vivid example of this kind of symbolic behavior in the boardroom and reinforces the (often) intentional view of this dilatory attitude: 'Postponing (or even killing) these decisions is often an intentional strategy [of directors] to eliminate risks [for them].' An independent director in several service industries stresses this assessment: 'Consultants or advisors are called in and this (using external help) is a classic way of saying no, of creating the "no" discourse. Broach an argument to let it fall. [It is] an elegant way of saying just no (because it is someone else who said it).' Another executive director provides an enlightening piece of evidence about this type of behaviors: 'I have heard exactly this at a board meeting: what we need here is to have someone else external (e.g. a relevant expert or a financial institution) saying no for us. Literally that.'

Along with centralizing decisions at board level, there is a trend in centralizing decisions *within* the board, as in centralizing decisions in the hand of CEOs/chairpersons. One of our interviewees suggests the label of 'coffee and cookies directors' in order to describe the situation of dominant top executives who feel particularly at ease with a meek and docile board. They expect the rest of the directorate 'to sip their coffee and eat butter cookies' while the first executive makes all the actual decisions.

For example, an executive chairman in the local subsidiary of a large firm reports: 'There is more work during crisis; there is no doubt about that. I have to drill down in issues I would not during expansion.' Another executive chairman, this time in the technology business, states: 'In the case I know better [this company] the board has been very involved in key decisions during the crisis period. I have myself wanted the board to explicitly know and authorize some key personnel exits [firings] both because of their importance [key people leaving] and the cost [in this case several million euros in severance costs due to termination] heavily impacting on results.'

Evidence from the field suggests mildly (but clearly) that two broad categories of CEO/chairperson emerge during crisis: dominant and participative. These types probably existed beforehand, but while they do not necessarily capture all the variance in CEO typologies, they become particularly visible during crisis, affecting board life in many ways (see Table 4.1). These CEO categories are possibly related to objective power indicators such as CEO duality or dominance (Finkelstein, 1992; Haleblian and Finkelstein, 1993), but particularly to psychological individual characteristics such as hubris (Hayward and Hambrick, 1997; Hayward, Rindova and Pollock, 2004).

Besides actual CEO/chairperson influence, final decision power is also contingent on other variables. For instance, board composition and degree of participation, or nature of ownership and company size, may facilitate this exertion of power—or, on the contrary, make it difficult. Thus, despite this centralization trend it is not always the chairperson who makes the final

TABLE 4.1   Data inferred typologies for Chairpersons/CEOs under crisis

Typologies of chairperson/ CEO	Evidence	Rationale
Dominant	'I know the case of a company, very big, with a very famous chairman. He told me he still doesn't know the tone of voice of some of the directors in his Board' (University Professor) 'This is the stereotype I have seen most: those who want to speak first and to be listened. The most dominant profile' (Independent Director)	Extreme typology of chairmen/CEOs in the exertion of power, likely related to duality, but also to personal character and company culture. These are those who want to dominate and do not expect push backs ('coffee and cookies' Chairman/CEO)
Participative	'There are those that may be because they are not confident or because they are balanced but know themselves and do not want to impose everything move to the other side: invite to participate and to discuss everything' (Executive Director) 'I have seen other leaders who are more able to delegate and want to involve people in their decisions' (Executive Director)	These are those who want to listen to other opinions and want everything under revision, whether because they feel unsure or because they are participative ('open minded' Chairman/CEO)

decision. An independent director in the financial industry explains this point: 'Of course, the chairperson is powerful (particularly when he/she is also executive director), but if directors insist together—no matter how convinced they are— they will be listened to.'

Another long-tenured independent director reflects on how company size and the dilution in stockholding and voting power, very often at par with firm size, also may be a variable involved in this exertion of power: 'In large companies, particularly in those where capital structure is less concentrated, executives are more able to exert their power.'

At times, the degree of participation of board members may influence the outcome of decisions. As an independent director in a manufacturing industry comments: 'It is not strange that, for instance, one throwing an idea or a name on the table in the first place may decisively influence the target for an acquisition.'

Strategies for centralization

From the above mentioned arguments and accounts, centralization seems to emerge as pattern-shaping information processing as well as decision-making processes at the top management level. We argue that the development of this pattern follows the emergence of practices as investigated by institutional theorists (Greenwood, Suddaby and Hinings, 2002; Lawrence, Suddaby and Leca, 2009). On one hand, this centralization pattern appears to be an outcome of environmental pressure characteristic of large economic crises. On the other hand, the centralization pattern appears to be the result of an intentional effort by board members and, in particular, by CEOs and chairpersons.

However, the structural argument of centralization as a pattern resulting from environmental pressures is left to significant macro-oriented studies of the sociology of organizations (e.g. new institutional theorists). Here we concentrate on a micro, more agent-centered view of the emergence of this centralization pattern, suggesting that intentional strategies for centralization are pursued by boards and board members in order to protect themselves from uncertainty risks.

Based upon our fieldwork, and as anticipated in Chapter 2, we have identified two main mechanisms for increased intervention and control leading to centralization: (a) an increased use of formal means in the way that the board operates (formalization), and (b) the creation of commissions and committees for the boards to dig into more operational domains (bureaucratization).

Formalization

The increased use of formal procedures in the operation of boards mainly touches on the board members' requests to trace and accurately record what happens during board meetings. This has increased, apparently, particularly in light of potential liabilities or reputational risks for directors, as well as due to the more general claim of transparency coming from the public and embodied in several institutionalized practices and norms.

There seems to be a number of motives for that trend. First, some of these formalized reactions are induced by regulatory pressures such as changes in the regulation of directors' responsibilities and liabilities, as well as due to legal or customary constraints to board composition, such as gender issues. In addition, corporate governance codes and recommendations proliferating from several sources globally also shape boards' daily job and drives towards more formalization.

Adoption of standardized practices enforced by regulations and norms reduces diversity of boards' processes, at least on the surface (Lounsbury, 2007). In many cases, formal adoption (of such practices) does not provoke in-depth changes of work practices but implies only a formal compliance to procedures. Nevertheless, the enforcement of standards usually occurs from a top-down perspective, reinforcing centralization of boards' decision-making within the organization. Moreover, as noted by several scholars (Power, 1996, among others), the adoption of these standards generates the task of managing them and promotes the role of auditors and controllers. Our interviewees have noticed the progressively growing importance of these professional groups within (or around) boards. At the same time, auditing and risk commissions have seen a steep increase in their effort during crisis, as reported by an independent director in a technological industry: 'There is a lot of work, more particularly in some board groups like the auditing committee.' An executive director in a large financial institution mentions it clearly: 'It might not have been totally caused by crisis but it [crisis] has helped gain a more substantive paper to auditing and nomination committees; they were just formal groups before, now they are far more important.'

Independently of external regulatory or institutional forces, a second group of causes in this formalization drift stems from organizational or individual reactions to a more complex or riskier environment. Indeed, crisis may increase risk aversion through accentuated fear towards pre-existing circumstances, for instance, legal liabilities for directors in case of organizational default or bankruptcy. An independent director still with executive responsibilities on other boards says: 'There is absolute horror during crisis to growing liabilities among directors.' Fear of responsibilities or penalties may have leveraged this formalization, as failure seems a closer and more likely outcome during crisis. An executive with responsibilities on several boards openly contends: 'It is more often than before that people mention explicitly that their opinion for or against should be specifically recorded in the board meeting minutes.'

A banker with board responsibilities in other industries suggests that there is risk aversion and self-interest involved: 'People are more concerned because, in the case of default, responsibility may go personally against directors and impending legal action might go against their own personal wealth.' While regulations regarding the personal liabilities of directors may differ across countries, the pressure is particularly felt by directorates during crisis: corporate failure becomes a more feasible result.

Board secretaries play a significant role in this formalization process, often recording arrangements reached outside the boardroom. The role of the board secretary (sometimes a non-director) is crucial in the formalization of the content and sequence of discussions during board meetings (even if, inexorably, the final mandate comes from the chairperson or CEO). As already suggested, part of this increased formalization may be due to individual self-protection or justification of position (Mayer and Gavin, 2005).

Bureaucratization

The second strategy to increase board (or CEO) intervention and control over decisions is related to the adoption of bureaucratic structures. Following the dynamic bureaucracy concept developed by Blau (1955), by bureaucratization we intend here the proliferation of formal units hierarchically dependent on the board, with specific tasks and reporting systems. Indeed, several board-related committees have emerged out of crisis, in theory to reduce workload for the board or the executive committee, or even to gain agility under crisis, but in fact increasing centralization and control at the organizational apex. In fact, these committees work to facilitate boardroom intervention in specific managerial domains.

While sometimes these structural changes are not formally communicated during crisis, frequently the reporting lines change, inducing a de facto organizational change to increase control and reduce managerial discretion (Marsh, 1992; Hage and Aiken, 1967). An executive director for a large global firm reports the following situation: 'We had an executive committee (EC), but it was not working and we are not using it any more. Now it is just me and the CEO, who meet when needed and follow up with the general management team (instead of using this EC).'

Other organizations, during crisis cost management or continuous improvement programs, have developed units with the sole (and, in principle, temporary) goal of reducing or controlling cost structures. Inevitably, this might have biased boardroom attention towards cost management and short-term-oriented targets. At times, these transitory units have not sufficiently integrated their cost reduction objectives into the global scorecard of the organization, thus putting their objectives at risk or falling into self-justification dynamics in order to perpetuate their own existence.

There are other board-related organizational entities emerging during crisis, many of them extracting decision-making power from other areas in the organization. For example, a coincident phenomenon, not always fully related to crisis, is the rise of new types of commissions (including those devoted to matters such as technology, sales or sustainability). They often reflect essential concerns and organizational reactions in front of crisis but, at the same time, affect traditional daily operations of other areas in the organization.

Advisory boards, with analogous functions to boards in strategy-making (but without risk of liabilities for their members), also have seen a steep increase in activity. One may suggest that this is an alternative way to attract managerial talent to assist executive management without exposing their members to potential legal liabilities, which is particularly attractive to them during crisis.

In parallel, splitting responsibilities is a common practice in many organizational settings allowing a more focused control; for instance, nominating and compensation committees are beginning to be conceived of as two separate committees rather than as one single committee. An expert in the corporate governance field explains this debate: 'It does not make much sense to have two critical functions like nomination and compensation under the same commission. To be fair, this should be two; those who decide on who, should not decide on how much.'

Centralization, together with intrinsic complexity of issues during crisis, leads to longer board meetings and frequently also to more recurrent board committee meetings, thus bringing an increased workload. The CEO of a large capital-intensive business agrees with this trend but sees this as a general phenomenon, not limited to a single commission, for instance those on risk: 'There is more work in commissions on all fronts, not only for those on risks during crisis.'

The increased workload of board committees' meetings is, in itself, a way to increase centralization because it offers the boardroom (and the board members) the renewed opportunity to drill down in mostly any matter and, thus, to influence the sequence and outcome of decision-making processes. As we have discussed, the board often takes this opportunity and increases its degree of influence in decision-making at a more operational level.

Drivers and implications of increased centralization and control during crisis

The main driver for the increased degree of centralization and control seems to be risk aversion. Increased risk aversion is a natural reaction to crisis because the latter implies, by definition, an increase in uncertainty and risk. A general manager (and CEO) describes this clearly: 'When things go well, there is no argument. Decision is not disputed. We want to dodge liabilities but you just cannot do that—that's dismissing responsibility. In political jargon, that means being "out of the power photo". Then, we generate a mess in collaboration with consultants and auditors. [We create] more complexity to reduce risks. More cost. Opportunities are lost and more mistakes emerge.'

There are a number of potential interpretations for this risk aversion. On the one hand, increased boardroom risk aversion may be a board reaction to reduce environmental ambiguity (Weick, 1969) or it might be simply a self-interested reaction (Williamson, 1975) because crisis generates more individual risks (legal, reputational) for each board member. While both motivations may be present, the previous passages more strongly support the second of these options. There are other converging views among our interviewees to support this. For example, a technology company chairman stated: 'Board members are often more concerned about themselves than about the (focal) company.'

The CEO in a large global firm suggests a compatible explanation: 'It is about misalignment of objectives and interests, particularly for independent directors. It is not that they are not capable or independent, but they pursue different things than the focal company. It is not, in practice, about maximizing value for the shareholder, but about minimizing personal risks and threats to reputation for them, in order to be member(s) of several boards and to be invited to new board memberships elsewhere.'

Strategies and mechanisms to increase centralization and control have several consequences and drawbacks. The centralizing process makes the board concentrate (or, to say the least, invest additional time) on less important priorities. This may also happen in some board committees focusing at times on relatively minor issues. As stated by the chairman of a large business services company: 'Then you end up having the board concentrated on how to reduce 17k euro travel spending in the German subsidiary; this is ridiculous and, even worse, it is crowding us executives out.' Indeed, those executives begin to delegate 'upwards' (to the board) some of their responsibilities (as in micromanagement). An independent director suggests that the logic for this upward influence is to avoid individual risks of potential mistakes: 'Everyone has done that. Taking up the ranks those things you don't see clearly so as to have everyone informed.'

Simultaneously to risk aversion, crisis also fosters lack of trust in people between the board of directors and the executive team. Indeed, extant literature has found several negative outcomes of firms that are declining, among them decreasing levels of trust and increasing levels of conflict (Cameron, Kim and Whetten, 1987; Cameron, Whetten and Kim, 1987). Trust is an essential component of a board, both in the initial composition of the team—for example, chairpersons or CEOs prefer to enroll directors with whom they have a previous relationship, strong references or common credentials or demography (see Westphal and Zajac, 1995)—and for subsequent working development. One of our interviewees, a long-standing director in several organizations, is very clear on this point: 'A key force for this centralization in the boardroom is mistrust in decision-making capability of subordinates (executives below).'

As already mentioned, a significant opportunity cost of these centralization and control mechanisms is indeed its influence on executive motivation. Certainly a well-balanced degree of centralization and control may prove healthy for the business (e.g. board of directors intervening to understand and provide advice, help or guidance to the executive team and later releasing control back to executives). However, too tight a control has several adverse implications. For instance, the relationship between the board of directors and/or any other board committee and the senior executive team may end up forming spirals of overload or, most frequently, procrastination in decision for the board and strong demotivation for the executive team ('vicious circles'). This might eventually lead to executive burnout and increased risk of attrition, with a resultant effect on board effectiveness.

A CEO in a company largely affected by the economic downturn bitterly complains about this 'control freak' attitude in the boardroom: 'Crisis spans agonies. It is difficult to be a chief executive when you share a board in which "no" is often on the table. It is clear for me that the board should monitor management. That is a noble task. The board should be vigilant and ask more or less incisively. But it should not be micro-management and very often now it is.' An independent director in several large companies describes the depressed mood of many executives during a process of crisis due to this excessive control: 'The management team begins to think "fire me or trust me" but stop driving me crazy and respect my freedom to act and decide.'

A graphical representation of this process of intervention and 'checkout' between the board and the senior management is presented in Figure 4.1.

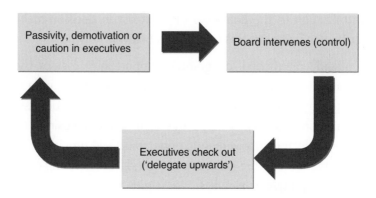

Risk aversion promotes upward delegation during crisis (e.g. people tend to 'rest' on their bosses to relieve their uncertainty, and those above mistrust them, leading to procrastination (or a spiral of effort) in all those above and demotivation and checkout on those below)

FIGURE 4.1 / Intervention–demotivation–checkout loop during crisis

Besides the frustration for executives, this intervention or micro-management mode elongates the decision-making process, postponing the actual decision and/or making it less effective. When there is no delay in decision, for instance due to the pressure of executives not to postpone action in the boardroom, the increased work overload for the board (more numerous or more difficult decisions, and more information to be analyzed in the same—or less—time) leads to a higher likelihood of mistakes. In other words, when the number of decisions to take is more, and the decisions required are tougher, decisions are either taken on time, but underutilizing relevant information or with less sound analysis and increasing odds for errors, or are postponed. Both outcomes are undesirable during crisis. An independent director in a large company states this clearly, showing that decisions might have been, at times, insufficiently reflected on: 'During crisis, there are more mistakes and more decisions that have to be "swallowed" six months later.'

Paradoxically, the underlying managerial assumption for this increased centralization seems to be that intervention and over-controlling may result in faster and better quality of decisions. As we described, in practice this does not necessarily hold true. In addition, as relevant literature has suggested (Harshbarger, 1971), centralized communication channels lead to more effective solutions with simple problems, while decentralized communication channels lead to more effective solutions with complex problems, as those fostered by crisis.

Consistently with this later contention, centralization has a clear downside, such as losses of business opportunity and increased decision-making delay. According to the managing director of a large service company, this is exactly the situation: 'Everyone finds a reason to ask for more information and further analysis; it is like Argentinean bolas;[1] eventually the issue is impossible to untie. It is a strategy, not necessarily conscious, to postpone (or not make) decisions.' The chairman of a financial institution explains: 'Everyone asks for more papers and more information. Everyone [on the board] speaks up now (particularly those who plan to say no). By asking for more information and more papers, decision is deferred and opportunity may be sometimes at risk.' An independent director in several private and public companies reports: '[In crisis] things are analyzed in more depth and more projects are rejected. It is a vicious circle. Management is demotivated and the growth of the company is castrated.'

---

[1]The Argentinean *bolas* is a throwing weapon used to capture running cattle (even if they are also used for game purposes). Similar weapons are known in other areas of the world such as Australia and Japan. They consist of two or more spherical balls (often made of stone or wood) on the ends of interconnected cords (usually made of braided leather). The weapon is normally used to entangle an animal's legs and make it fall (or even break some bones). The crux of the metaphor here is the entanglement between the cords and the animal's legs.

He concludes: 'Boards [in the case of crisis] castrate growth, management control emphasis is increased; growth is limited and so is the evolution of the company. That could really kill the company.'

In sum, the overall lesson so far is that the boardroom shifts focus in front of perceived (enacted) crisis. An increased degree of centralization and control takes the driver's seat, increasing the workload and cost of deciding, and often postponing strategic decision-making activity and/or harming its quality.

We are now moving towards the inner circle of decision-making. The next step is to present a further understanding of the micro-mechanisms of how boardroom decisions are made during crisis, and to take a closer look at descriptions, causes and implications of crisis-induced decision-making mechanisms. Parochialism seems to be a key factor.

5

Parochialism and Conflict in the Boardroom during Crisis: Does Ransom Make it Random?

To make it clear at the outset of this chapter, decision-making as a rational process is not what we are about to describe. This does not mean that we believe, as harsh critics of management, that decision-making processes do not have a strong rationale. They do, but that rationale is not always and not necessarily related to what theory or well-intentioned observers might expect from decision makers at the top.

Organizational interest and stewardship often have to compete with actors' self-interest to the extent that, particularly during crisis, this opportunist self-interest—under the form of status, power and compensation, to name just three basic and common motives—is intensified and more often collides with organizational interest. This blurs the limits between what seems logical and chaotic in the midst of crisis.

This chapter is devoted to describing such a situation. Whilst this account aims to be as accurate as possible it is by no means theoretically neutral. We made the explicit decision to follow a precise theoretical view to orient our description and root it in the existing academic debate.

Despite boardrooms being hierarchical settings, due to the CEO or chairperson's formal power, we look at boards from a non-hierarchical decision-making perspective: the garbage-can model of choice (Cohen, March and Olsen, 1972). Decisions under conflicting goals (individual versus group, public versus concealed, explicit versus implicit) have been described in several studies through the garbage-can model of choice lenses (see, among others, Cohen and March, 1974; 1986; March and Olsen, 1976; March and Weissinger-Baylon, 1986; March, 1988). The garbage-can model of choice aims at theorizing organized anarchies,[1] which are defined (Cohen, March and Olsen, 1972) as organizational forms sharing three main characteristics: (a) unclear preferences, (b) unclear technologies and (c) fluid participation.

With regard to the first characteristic, preferences are problematic; organizations act according to a variety of inconsistent or uncertain preferences. This is particularly true during crisis, as in such a situation it is tougher to select what the main goals should be. As we shall see, boards do not always have a clear or steady set of ideas about what they are trying to achieve. Their goals are often sparse and contradictory. In other words, our cognition limits are more significant when facing crisis, so it is more complex for us to select and prioritize our choices.

With regard to the second characteristic, technology is unclear; organizational processes are not fully understood by participants

---

[1] It is beyond the scope of the volume to provide a detailed account of the garbage-can model and its theoretical and empirical developments. For an updated overview, see Lomi and Harrison (2012).

and 'trial and error' affects the collective output. Even the adoption of new technologies occurs following unstable patterns, and available technology constantly changes. Uncertainty emerges on what should be the proper way of running organizational processes.

Turning to the third characteristic, participation is fluid; as participants vary in the amount of time and energy devoted to different activities, their involvement varies from one time to another. Since each participant in the decision-making process bears her/his own set of preferences and cognitive approaches, fluid participation makes instability diffuse and determines a context in which preferences, goals interpretations and cognition are in constant change.

Both 'trial and error' and 'fluid participation' seem to prevail during crisis. The original arguments developed by James March stated that the garbage-can model was intended to frame the way that organizations cope with the highest level of uncertainty and ambiguity. That condition reflected the environmental turbulence and economic crisis of the early 1970s (the first oil shock). Without entering into historical comparisons—which are far beyond the scope of this book— we can argue that the impact of that crisis on organizational processes and decision-making can be considered as remarkable as the one we are experiencing now.

The decisional outcome in the garbage-can model of choice is related to the temporal connection between issues, actors, solutions and (decision) choices, rather than to the rational sequence of problems-setting, solution-finding and problem-solving. This is exactly what our interviewees observed during crisis: logics of opportunity and appropriateness, rather than pure economic rationality, rules problem-solving in such a decision setting. As the chairman of a technology company states: 'Things try to follow the logical sequence of problem identification, data-gathering and generation of solution options, but phases are seldom that rigid.' Another interviewee, the executive chairman of a large energy company, states: 'Existing information conditions the decision. The decision-making process is more circular than linear. There are seldom clear-cut choices. In the process of gathering information, the decision or action is implicitly approached (and what options to take or abandon).'

In the following sections of this chapter we try to describe the main elements of decisions, namely the issues at hand, the actors (independent/non-executive directors,[2] proprietary directors, CEOs/chairpersons), their context and limitations, and the decision-making processes during crisis observed through the lenses of the garbage-can model of choice.

The issues

We have argued that during crisis there are more decisions to take or, at least, there is more decision workload. We also contended that decisions under crisis are often more important because, in addition to all decisions to run a business (such as purchasing, sales, finance, human resources, etc.), there are specific crisis-induced decisions (such as restructuring and other corporate activity). Thus, timeliness of decision becomes more crucial than ever. There are more issues and they are more pressing but, as mentioned earlier, there is often more management information available in order to reduce uncertainty in decision-making.

---

[2] We use independent/non-executive as equivalent terms, even if, at least in theory, all directors should be independent.

The political task of the board of directors' members includes the way that management information is used within the decision-making process. The use of management information by boards strongly affects the quality of decisions. We have found two common groups of limitations. The first one pertains to the quality of managerial information provided by the focal company to board members and its timeliness. The second is related to the actual preparation (or dedication) of directors to board activity, such as board meetings and commissions.

Within the first group of limitations in the use of management information there may be, for instance, biases in the way that information is gathered. According to one of our interviewees, an executive director: 'The way information is gathered is often non-neutral. Because in the way information is gathered the solution is often implicit.' Such bias due to the search set may increase risks of decision bias (Tversky and Kahneman, 1974).

Frequently, the information packages provided to directors are not properly balanced. They contain too much or too little information or are untimely. In the words of an independent director with a very long tenure in senior political and managerial positions: 'Why the hell do we need the deviation in raw material x consumption for product y in factory z in Germany? This is useless for a director; it makes you lose focus on the most important things.' Another executive director states: 'The quality and depth of information provided to directors on many boards in some countries in Europe is just fair, when not scarce, compared to that provided in most Anglo or American settings. Just a "pass".' The chairman of a large technology firm provides a more personal interpretation on this issue: 'There are executives who don't really believe in the usefulness of boards, and boards are (should be) to help management lead the business.' He continues: 'When this happens, these executives devote little time to this [boardroom work]. And when they do, they believe it is just a necessary evil.'

Timeliness of information during crisis is also of the essence. However, the lead time with which this information is provided to directors is not always the most appropriate; sometimes information is provided too short in advance, which is particularly harmful during crisis. A former CEO in the financial industry reports: 'This depends a lot on the company. Some [firms] provide a good set of information with enough lead time (and many of them even have a micro site/web specifically tailored for their board), some just do not care.'

There is a second group of shortcomings related to the actual degree of involvement and preparation of directors for their boardroom activity. For example, the use that board members make of the information provided by the firm affects decisively the final quality of decision. Even if practices vary by country, the dedication of time invested by directors in the preparation of boards appears at times limited, also for large listed companies (PWC, 2011), particularly when they have other executive responsibilities (such as CEO in a different company) or serve in multiple directorates. This is relevant because, as we have already argued, busy boards might be less effective in monitoring management performance (Fich and Shivdasani, 2006).

The chairman in a very large multinational business provides severe self-criticism: 'Little preparation plus little effort and few board meetings end up in little rigor in decision.' There is agreement with that contention in the words of an independent director: 'If the information is too little, or too much, and it is not well prepared because we do not devote time enough ... then this is useless ... It is much better to receive just a fair amount of information, relevant to the issues at hand, and prepare it well.'

Context, actors and limitations

Undeniably, decision-making becomes particularly vital during crisis. As we reported in previous chapters, the debate leading to decision intensifies, both substantively (as in there are frequently more numerous and more complex issues) and emotionally (in that it is infused with more tension). The context in which decisions are taken is affected by this increased tension, idiosyncratic of crisis.

The balance between conflicting priorities of the different actors at the top is hard to attain. During crisis it seems often more difficult for the board to remain cohesive as a team and to balance all goals, due to the suspended 'strength' of existing rules or procedures (see for example; Weick, 1993). An independent director in a large international firm provides a graphic metaphor to describe these behaviors: 'A board during crisis is sometimes like a cricket nest (a birdcage)...'.

Self-interest of individuals grows during crisis because resources are inadequate or insufficient to cope with the situation (Starbuck and Hedberg, 1977; Webb, 1994). In the words of an executive in a financial firm seriously hit by the current economic crisis, the situation becomes particularly tense: 'Sadly, crisis often extracts the worst and most predatory behaviors of everyone, the worst of human beings.'

That said, people seem to avoid confrontation if they can. For example, directors do not overtly and visibly resist chairpersons or key executive directors, except if the decision may seriously and irremediably harm the directors's personal reputation or prestige. Our interpretation is that, by doing so, directors behave in a sort of 'tit for tat' or equivalent retaliation strategy (Axelrod, 1984) because the actual cost of a fully opportunist behavior may affect them later (e.g. social punishment within the focal board and/or within a highly connected environment: directors often sit on more than one board).

An independent director explains: 'There are always conversations behind the scenes but [there are] much more now.' Another independent director reports: 'There are telephone calls, lunches, dinners and conversations. You just cannot enter the board meeting without knowing what the rest think about an issue.'

Thus, as our interviewees suggest, political maneuvering and coalition-building become more important under crisis. There are more moves (shortcuts and workarounds) behind the scenes to coordinate individual interests and group targets (for instance, to balance group cohesion and focal organization's interests). This fosters a more loosely coupled connection between decisions and outcomes.

Hence, all boardroom actors devise their strategies to balance all interests, when possible. Every actor maneuvers to avoid risk on some goals critical to them (such as compensation, position, role, effort, return on investment, etc.). A clear risk of mismatching appears between a boardroom's theoretical objectives (such as being the watchdog of management and the defender of shareholders) and those of individual actors and the collective outcome of the board as a whole. Unclear and fuzzy preferences emerge from the clash among board and individual goals shaping actors' strategies for decision during crisis. We shall now look at decisions from the perspectives of the different participating groups within the board: proprietary directors, independent directors and CEOs/chairpersons.

Proprietary directors

Proprietary directors (owners of a significant stake of the business, or other directors representing their interests in the boardroom) devise their own strategies in the face of crisis, with the prevailing interest of protecting owners' investment: they often prioritize their own interest to the one of the focal organization. As the executive chairman in a technology start-up reports:

> Nature of stockholder is important (open market, institutional, PEs [private equity firms] etc.) because it may change the way that the board of directors act (focus on the short term versus long term); for example, PEs only think in terms of pure short-term P&L [profit and loss], and often forget about organic or human-side considerations of the decisions taken but, in any case, all owners often bring their personal state of mind to the board.

Proprietary directors (or owners) often exert their influence via vote and/or veto powers in order to decide what the key topics are. This is particularly intensified when they amass (or represent) large stakes of the business. The CEO in a very large family conglomerate puts it this way: 'Typically it is owners or proprietary directors who propose the key topics *also* during crisis' (emphasis added).

Owners or proprietary directors induce considerable pressure to executives, regardless of the crisis context, or precisely because of it, at a high cost in terms of personal erosion and suffering for executives. An executive board member bitterly complains: 'All other businesses—even those they [proprietary directors] manage directly—have lost 30 to 40 percent of their volumes during this crisis, but when it comes to the companies they [proprietary directors representing owners, or owners themselves] participate in on the board, they blame everything on the executives.' He continues: 'Sometimes (more in crisis) proprietary directors bring their own issues to the company and are more interested in their own fortunes rather than in the (focal) company. Proprietary directors are a blatant issue by themselves during crisis; they are part of the problem more than the solution.'

This pressure is even stronger (and entails increased potential risk for the organization) when there are few executives or just one (such as the CEO) in the directorate. A chairperson in a large global business, and with international experience in several industries, describes this situation: 'It is more difficult to be balanced in the boardroom, and vision will be more biased by the (limited) executive view, when there are few executives on the board (usually only one, the CEO). That is a terrible governance risk in some companies.' In addition to that, the attitude of independent directors does not always contribute to offset this pressure, as we shall see below.

Independent directors

Hidden dynamics of the board acting against effective board independence may be significant (Westphal, 1998). This is particularly notable during crisis, because there is more tension for the CEO or chairperson, slack is reduced and the number of available courses of action becomes smaller. Not surprisingly, our informants report that, during crisis, independent directors pursue predominantly their main self-interest: preserving roles and status.

This is understandable. Being an independent director, particularly for a large company, is attractive—at least at first sight—although risk can be considerable. First, there is a notable social appreciation for the role. In addition, nominal compensation for directors in large companies can be fairly high (see for example PWC, 2011 focused on Spain, but identifying fairly common cross-national evidence; HKP, 2012; The Guardian, 2013a). Country differences notwithstanding (see, for example, evidence of relatively high compensation in Spain and other countries reported by Sánchez-Marín, Baixauli-Soler and Lucas Perez, 2010; HKP, 2012), independent directors generally do not want to lose their status: it is often a key component of their individual branding.[3] An external independent expert in the formal regulations and informal practices of the corporate governance field confirms this assessment: 'The number one nightmare for a director is to get the sack. Therefore, they do whatever it takes to stay on board.' An independent director with a long tenure in board memberships worldwide describes this dilemma: 'It is tough biting the hand of the one helping you be there. This does not facilitate independence.'

The previous passages crudely reveal that there is often little stimulus for real independence. Mechanisms for board access, together with some other factors affecting actual independence (such as the alignment between board evaluation and compensation), are circumstances that already existed before the current financial crisis. However, they do not strengthen voice or risk-taking attitudes in the boardroom, often necessary to face increased complexity of issues during crisis.

This does not preclude that there are, of course, truly independent directors in the boardroom, but it gets more difficult to play an independent role within boards during crisis. According to our field research, we have seen two types of forces against independence on the board: those internal to the company and those that are institutional.

Internally, within the focal company, there may be barriers in the form of inner pressures from the chairperson/CEO, particularly when this is aligned with a significant portion in ownership. One of our interviewees, an executive director, provides a vibrant example of this situation: 'Our chairperson was really angry because a group of independent directors had not followed

---

[3] In Italy, for example, it is not unusual for a top manager to sit at the same time on ten boards of both corporations and state-owned organizations.

her will. The Chairperson complained bitterly about how much money the company was paying them every year (and had paid them over the years) and that they were not "helping" and for once we needed them to do so. The Chair was very cross and did not really understand that they were doing the right thing, exactly what they were paid for: defending what they thought was right for the company (as a whole), rather than behaving as yes-men. They are not employees.'

As is already well known in boardroom literature (Westphal and Stern, 2007), a common strategy to survive on the board is ingratiation with powerful peers such as proprietary directors and/or the chairperson/CEO; less frequently with other independent directors, except if these are very close to powerful executives or significant shareholders. An independent director provided us with a vivid portrait of these moves:

> Talking (on the aisles and turfs) is always important. But in crisis, politics is even more important. Inevitably there is more tension; there is more discussion and there are more political twists in all processes. During the breaks within the board meetings, people talk about what everyone's going to vote, about the defense of interests and the best interest of everyone; while when things go well, people devote break time to flattery and to say how amazing this company is.

At times, these ingratiatory moves—reflecting forces against independence—are related to the social pressure of 'social or customary' etiquette ('the way we do things around these settings'). As a former executive director (now independent director) mentions: 'Independent directors never confront executive directors; rather than that, they convey their points through proprietary directors.' An executive director with a long tenure on boards of large corporations assumes implicitly (and naturally) that this is the right pattern of behavior in the boardroom: 'Independent directors do not take the lead on the debate not even during crisis, *obviously*' (emphasis added). In sum, independent directors have frequent difficulties to take the lead on board debates: putting their position at stake entails political risk for them.

From the institutional perspective of the market of corporate directors, the situation is not very different; there are often strong forces making independence more problematic. Independence is not easy, either, as it is not socially fostered due to the large embeddedness (Granovetter, 1985) of these (interlocking) settings (Mizruchi, 1996). In other words, the community of board members is small and interconnected enough to promote the appropriate behaviors through the sentence of unsuitable initiatives and the circulation of information related to the alignment of board members with customary rules. To put it plainly, social 'noise' (unwanted notoriety), does not help to create a long-standing career as an independent director. So directors often see their independence co-opted in the larger community of board members, usually from the very moment they access the position. An independent director cynically declares: 'If you do not make mistakes, you are safe and have the opportunity to reach other directorates (and make prestige and money for you).' Another independent director goes even further in this plausible misalignment between incentives and behavior: 'If you do not obey, you're out and this can be a lot of money.'

The importance of the network formed by board members is well acknowledged by corporations in terms of connectedness potential and social capital of directors. Conforming to taken-for-granted community norms is a key reference to aim at a central position in the network. An external expert in the corporate governance field observes: 'Some large, international headhunters mention this is not always a rigorous and transparent process; companies are often much more concerned about social and market connections of potential directors rather than by their actual talent (management stature or experience) as candidates; and there should be more balance between those two dimensions.'

Coeteris paribus, risks for independent directors due to increased uncertainty, complexity and political pressures seem higher during crisis. Therefore, if they remain on board, being truly independent requires even more maturity and courage than before (assuming it was already not easy before to do well as an independent director). The maturity and capacity of directors turn out to be even more fundamental during crisis. An independent director explains this tension: 'Divergence in the boardroom? Yes, I have personally suffered the open discrepancy between proprietary directors [or owners] and independent directors. Yes. I have suffered from this a lot. I had very bad times. I don't want to and I cannot speak about this ... Not only in crisis. In crisis it also may be. Yes. [He stops and thinks.] Crisis can amplify differences. For instance, if for any other reason some of the directors (such as a significant owner in the company) have a need for cash and the focal company may contribute to solve it (for example, through a dividend decision).'

An executive director in a large company states: 'I don't really think it is a real problem of independence if you are talking about real good independent directors. The real tension is between independent and proprietary (or, at times, executive) directors when there is crisis and there are absolutely opposed criteria. Those real large conflicts are because of the polarization between those two groups with different interests. Really independent directors just don't want to see their names on the cover page of the press the following day.' He continues: 'Then, with real big names in independent positions, the adjusting mechanism is not shutting their mouths up; that's not possible, so they are doomed to leave.'

Thus, the possibility for independent directors to influence boards seems to be more at stake during crisis. On the one hand, pressures towards less independence increases for those directors who want to keep their status and position. On the other hand, room to influence boards shrinks for independent directors willing to contribute with their third-party views. Both dynamics are highly counterproductive for crisis management, when ideas for fresh action can be crucial for recovery. In the words of an executive director working for a global leader in a capital intensive industry: 'Most [independent directors] are independent, but misaligned. I mean, they don't share objectives (theirs is actually avoiding damage to personal reputation) with the companies in which they serve. I am pretty sure that in good times there is a notable increase in the presence of independent directors. In bad times, transparency indexes—and the independent ratio—plummet. They [independent directors] are a real nuisance when there can be different criteria.'

Not surprisingly, and besides ingratiation, independent directors use several hedging strategies to defend position or reduce personal risk: they look for legal help, advisory services or insurance. Indeed, looking for civil insurance to cover responsibilities is more frequent than before. An independent director attests: 'For sure, coverage for civil and responsibility insurances have grown.' The former CEO in a large global financial institution adds: 'You can bet about this, that insurance policies' coverage has grown. People ask overtly [how to be covered]. What would happen if …? This has implications in the way decisions are made because people are more worried.' Finally, the chairman in a financial institution provides his own prescription to reach more board independence, particularly for independent, external directors: 'There should be a number of limits for independent directors, for instance in age, length of service and compensation. Otherwise, it is very difficult to behave like a real independent director.'

As mentioned in a previous chapter, another tactic that directors use—particularly but not exclusively independent directors—is formalizing everything (or as much as possible) in order to gain certainty on the agreements and positions of everyone and to reduce their own perception of risk. Of course, this is not always an easy strategy, because it might mean taking an uncomfortable stance in front of other colleagues in the boardroom and, very particularly, in front of the CEO or chairperson, which—as we have already suggested—is often fatal for long-term tenure on the board.

In sum, the odds of losing status and exit (for independent directors) are probably higher under crisis. Obviously, not everyone can be a good independent director. An executive director in a private equity business states: 'Those who most showed off their roles were often those who first got scared and voluntarily left. There are examples of independent directors leaving their roles abruptly because of the risk of increasing liabilities. Sometimes losing "names" does not impoverish the board; conversely, with less "known" names there may be a better board team.'

Despite all these pressures on directors we just described, the total directors' attrition rate was not high at the time of the assessment in the sample of companies in our research: not in excess of 10 percent yearly, including all motives and all type of directors. A likely explanation is that crisis had not yet imposed a significant effect on composition at the time of the field work. Another competing explanation is related to the significant burden of changes in the boardroom; for example, for larger and specifically for listed companies, a board member leaving the role may have a significant public relations impact. Besides the potential effect on stock prices, the departure of a director requires external communication (to the regulator, as well as careful and targeted communication to the environment). In such a situation, communication to the media and to the larger investment community is also customary.

The chairperson and/or CEO

Admittedly, some chairpersons/CEOs are interested as much in their responsibility as they are in preserving their role or 'saving face'. Consistent with the literature (Westphal and Stern, 2006; 2007) our interviewees confirm that some of them seem to look for obedience and adulation. An independent director with experience in several industries describes this need for flattery that some leaders have: 'The role I have seen more often is the chairman who speaks, the one who wants to be listened to and asks the rest to speak later. But there are good leaders and I have seen some. The style of the first executive is very often a stamp for the team.'

Some others use symbolism to legitimate self-interest (Westphal and Zajac, 1994; Zajac and Westphal, 1995). A former CEO mentions the following: 'Very recently (during the crisis) some very important executives have deceived their stockholders by saying they were reducing their severance or parachute packages limiting them to just "x" years. But at the same time, they were significantly pumping up their long-term compensation plans (e.g. pension funds or similar retirement benefits) in a much bigger amount.'

Besides those objective power factors stated in the literature on dominant CEOs (Haleblian and Finkelstein, 1993) or the ego-puffery feeding hubristic or narcissistic CEOs (Hayward, Rindova and Pollock, 2004; Chatterjee and Hambrick, 2007), there are some other reasons that ease their action under crisis. For example, due to their role, they have more critical management information at hand, particularly in the case of dual CEOs (being also chairperson of the board). Thus, under crisis, chairpersons/ CEOs often devise their strategies from this dominant situation (such as privileged access to key management information), encouraging board participation to preserve role and 'share' accountability. Indeed, stated independence is not the same as real independence, and the risk of these practices is often purely formal box-ticking, without substantive implementation of good governance practices (OECD, 2010).

At the same time, chairpersons/CEOs are equally sensitive to increased personal risk (such as legal liabilities and/or the risk of being fired). Therefore, during crisis they follow new-fangled strategies both outside and inside the boardroom. During crisis they act as 'political equilibrium makers' more than as managers, and some see and even actually describe their own role that way. This implies more work on their side, both in front and behind the scenes, and a tighter interaction with the rest of the board. For instance, chairpersons/CEOs foster new opportunities for meetings (for example offsite and ad hoc board meetings and retreats to cover a certain set of issues, such as strategy or to extend board discussions, for instance to discuss risk topics. An executive director with a long international tenure acknowledges more activity of this type: 'It was less frequent before to organize offsite strategy meetings, but now we do it.'

During crisis the CEO-boardroom reporting pattern seems to change. Top leaders move from reporting mainly by exception to reporting almost every step, most likely influenced by this increased perception of risk. They follow a number of paths to increase reporting: they do it more frequently and at their discretion; and they tend to report those decisions that help create a tighter rapport with their board and, very particularly, those riskier decisions. In the words of an independent director in several private firms: 'CEOs often promote this increased participation of stockholders during crisis, e.g. to create rapport with them and dilute responsibilities.' Another independent director says: 'The CEO reports more frequently to the board and thus releases her tension and feels more comfortable.' In sum, our interpretation is that CEO reporting varies in respect to having everyone involved and building consensus, even if such an approach may involve a higher risk of herding at the board (Banerjee, 1992).

Undeniably, these strategies of chairpersons/CEOs under crisis to tackle board issues make them devote much more time and energy to these topics than during expansion. Outside the boardroom, they do more extensive searches of information and perform a closer scrutiny to business. For instance, more questioning is frequent and more one-to-one conversations exist; both publicly and privately, not simply to influence but to elicit ideas. Another interviewee, an independent director in the financial services industry, tells us: 'I don't know if I can say that so openly, but I feel CEOs tend to ask for feedback and suggestions more genuinely during crisis.' Eventually, top executives make deeper dives, participating in decisions they would not approach during expansion. This is part of the information-processing centralization we discussed earlier (Gibbons, 2003) even if it may be also genuine interest in other directors' opinions, triggered by their own increased risk aversion.

We believe there are interesting similarity points between boards and top teams in the political arena under crisis. After all, the role of boards is managing complexity, the same thing a government team should do. Two top executives give their view on this same topic. The chairperson in a large infrastructure global business says: 'A CEO during crisis is a political actor, making arrangement with all parties all day.' The chairperson (and CEO) of a large B2B business gives his view: 'More time was devoted by the CEO to the board issues (probably to build more consensus) while in the expansion times, it was more about persuasion.'

Indeed, building consensus and motivation around board members captures more time from the CEO's/chairperson's schedule. This political-like stance implies that not everything is internal in these changes in behavior. There are significant external activities to take care of, particularly for large listed companies. External communication is crucial. The chairperson of a large retail firm says: 'Particularly for large listed companies, during crisis external communication to several stakeholders becomes central for the CEO/chairperson.' A former politician with strong corporate experience adds: 'A very well-known politician, who worked directly with Mr. X [president of a country's government], told me that there are very clear similarities between government teams and top management teams, except that public exposure is often much more erosive for politicians [than for managers].' This difference may be evened during crisis in which the public eye and external communication are more important than ever before for board members, particularly for the chairperson or CEO. This analogy with the political arena has already been the object of attention by Gavetti, Levinthal and Ocasio (2007) and is raising further academic interest, especially in Europe, where the osmosis between corporate and political careers is becoming common.

The decision-making process during crisis

Although boardroom meetings are not the only decision settings for the board, the nature and intensity of debate in the boardroom during crisis represent the core of the decision-making process. Intensity of debate is intrinsically related to the number and complexity of issues. Thus, even if there are still company differences often induced by typologies and characters of their top executives, the debate on the board is often more intense during crisis and implies more and more difficult work.

Moreover, some mild signs of self-criticism (such as self-assumption of the responsibility of boards in the onset of crisis) appear, fostering a more rigorous debate. An independent director in several industries reports: 'There is a clear causal factor of crisis in board behavior.' An independent director in the financial industry observes: 'This is a very particular crisis; really deep and long; things that worked before, do not now. Before it [part of board discussions] was just red tape, but now there are more substantive discussions.' This is coupled with an increased awareness of the importance of their roles, something we mentioned earlier in Chapter 2. An independent director with a long international tenure admits: 'If only we had done things then the same way we do now, odds are that this crisis would be smaller.' In a similar vein, an independent director with a long executive experience states: 'I think that boards are far more important now than they were in expansion: in expansion it was about making more or making less money, but now it is about survival.' He continues: 'A weak board is a real risk under crisis, particularly for large listed companies.'

The nature of board meetings changes when debate is more intense. The former interviewee reports this same idea: 'Regarding board dynamics, no doubt meetings are longer and debates are more intense, much more. More important and intense debates are related to strategic plans and budgeting. All is under revision. Debates are much ampler (everything is under scrutiny).'

Inevitably, some examples of low intensity of debate still exist where dominant executive or board coalition cools down the intensity of discussion. This may lead to create a 'cohort' effect (that is, groupthink or herding) and ultimately drive worse quality of decision. Confirming this risk, an independent director within a private company assesses sadly: 'The intensity of debate has not changed (increased) enough during crisis.' Likewise, a former CEO in the onset of crisis in a European-headquartered company states: 'There are boards in which there is still no debate on important things and it is only concentrated on board renewal, compensation and salaries; but much less on actual governance.'

If there is lack of debate, board effectiveness during crisis is even more difficult if the board is not cohesive enough or board capacity (such as composition or skills) or team size is not adequate. There is some evidence in extant literature of the effect on team effectiveness of team size (Poulton, 1995; Sharma and Ghosh, 2007) even if now more conclusive (Wheelan, 2009). An independent director with a long executive career addresses explicitly this point: 'I see no point in those large boardrooms with many people; that is useless.' The president of a technology company reports: 'It is impossible to manage a board larger than 15.' Even if, in principle, the number of members is a broad indication of the capacity and effectiveness of the board, as a rule of thumb it is unlikely that a group in excess of 10 (or 12) people can be completely effective.

As provocatively remarked by one of our interviewees, a significant question about the nature of board debate, and not specifically during crisis times, is to ask if boards really take decisions. They do, but apparently not always and not everything in terms of the decision-making process happens in the boardroom meetings: as we have already seen, the boardroom meeting is just the last mile in the decision-making process. An independent director says: 'Key decisions (such as major acquisition) are sometimes precooked. But somehow this is logical. You cannot decide something important without previous work, analysis, etc.' Everything is often settled outside of boardroom settings. In the words of an executive director in several capital intensive firms: 'There is a golden rule. Nothing is decided in the boardroom. You never take anything to the board meeting that you are not 100 percent sure is going to be accepted. Those are the real issues for CEOs, and when there may be a serious problem or conflict.'

Finally, crisis is more emotionally loaded. Increased tension and emotionality are inherent to tough times (Gladstein and Reilly, 1985). Indeed, a decision is not always the outcome of boardroom decision-making processes; or, to say the least, it is not the only outcome. Besides good or bad decisions, tension seems to be a clear and mostly invariable outcome of boardroom decision-making under crisis. We will now consider which are the main drivers behind this increased tension in the boardroom.

The structural factors behind tension

Diverging interests and logical asymmetries among board members in the access to information are among the main causal factors behind tension in the boardroom. First, for instance, there are logical information asymmetries (such as access to management information) between executive directors and the rest (executive directors versus non-executive directors, executive committee and the rest). An independent director with a long tenure as an executive states critically: 'Only executives and (very seldom) some independent directors have real knowledge of the company. Sometimes they (generally, external or independent directors) know less about us than the external market or industry analysts following the company.' Recently, a comparable argument has been suggested by Martin (2011) to criticize actual effectiveness of independent directors.

There are several other structural sources of power asymmetry. For example, there are differences in voting power when there are block-holdings, those with a controlling stake in the ownership of the company, often in the 5 percent to 50 percent range, and with a long-term ($\geq$ 3 years) interest (Bogert, 1996). Thus, the dominant role of proprietary directors (or owners) frequently acts as the igniter of the analysis process of a given decision. As has already been suggested in this chapter, the objectives of proprietary directors and firms may at times—and particularly during crisis—collide (for example, protecting their own investment value versus best company interest) and this creates tension. The chairperson of a large financial institution offers a clear example of this contradiction: 'Some months ago, there was an investment opportunity, but some shareholders had no money and others did. Not by lucky chance, those that did not have enough money to invest in the new venture (or those who had more difficult access to funding) saw many more "objective" issues with the opportunity, while they were actually defending their position not to dilute their control power in the company.'

Another example of these structural differences increasing tension is the case of fragmented and confronting ownership (for example, two or more large competing shareholders/shareholder groups especially when there is no block-holding to control the board). There are many recent examples of the tension in the boardroom that is derived from these types of situation (for example, *The Independent*, 2013; *Financial Times*, 2011a; *Financial Times*, 2012). Less frequently, it is the executive director who controls the board; and a significant shareholder sees their influence reduced because of executives protecting existing composition of the board.

The internal and process factors behind tension

In addition to structural factors (and their obvious consequences for board processes), there are specific internal and process dynamics affecting increased tension during crisis.

For example, composition is important in that character and competence of members affect TMT (board) outcome (Hambrick and Mason, 1984). An executive chairperson nicely expresses this idea: 'There are people at any board that, even when they are agreeing, they create conflict, and there are others that even when denying something, make everyone feel good.' An independent director theorizes on the same idea: 'A board is a small group and there are lots of things that are depending on personalities, rather than on ideas.'

Dynamics and interaction are contingent on personalities and participation. Egos have a critical role in board processes. In the words of an independent director in several financial institutions: 'We are not talking now about management any more, but about psychology and groups: egos are the key.'

Mutual trust is central for an effective board during crisis and, if we assume the former, then composition affects the process. In the words of a former CEO, now independent director in several companies: 'You [the CEO or chairperson] have to learn to trust in your team to keep this working.' Building trust is essential for board process effectiveness. Several other process factors contribute to this tension. For example, regardless of the quality of existing relationships, individual actors' goals may collide and generate tension under crisis. An independent director in several organizations reports exactly this: 'No matter how good previous relationships are, inevitably there will be increased tension among board members during crisis.' Differences in individual risk aversion, together with a more difficult balance—when not open confrontation—between self and shared interests, plus increased politics on the board (such as coalitions) inevitably leverage tension. An independent director with several large companies says: 'There is a significant difference in behavior; all is more politically loaded during crisis; all is flattery during bullish phases. But there is a lot of politics in crisis.'

During crisis, there is more at stake, sometimes the survival of the firm—very often the position and reputation of everyone in the boardroom. Consequently, and regardless of the actual composition, during crisis most often the degree of participation in the boardroom increases, as people who did not participate actively before now do. Indeed, effective participation was not always the rule in the pre-crisis situation. An independent director with a very long tenure both in private and public organizations provides an example of this behavior: 'I was on the board with someone (a proprietary director) who had a well-formed criterion over most subjects and he spoke openly about almost any issue everywhere, except in boardroom meetings. I have never ever heard him say a single word (in board meetings) except hello and goodbye.' Another interviewee, an independent director in several listed companies, asserts: 'I always speak. But this is not always the case. There are people who never speak. I have a dumb, but clear example of this behavior: we may find an acronym in the documentation provided to the board and we do not know what it means. And, in order not to lose face, no one dares to ask. I always do.' Likewise, the former CEO of a large financial institution states: 'A good director has to say what he thinks, always. That (saying what one honestly thinks) is the main reason to stay there.'

Even mere presence in the boardroom heavily influences discussion and intensity of participation. 'I am pretty sure', says an independent director, 'that some decisions might have been different in the outcome—and for sure totally in the process—had there been different people who attended that specific meeting.'

There are several other process factors conditioning inner life at the boardroom during crisis, some of them subtle but still important because of this increased tension. An important one in crisis dynamics is mood and morale. Baseline mood changes: such as board members becoming depressed, sad or even aggressive. For instance, executives may be under more stress, or proprietary directors or owners may see their fortunes at increased risk. This is clearly described in the words of the chairperson and CEO of a large European company: 'Mood is debacle. You have to encourage people and tell them that the world is not over. It is not about justifying, it is about surmounting this situation, not complaining about it.'

Finally, attention to non-verbal and body language is always important, but it is even more crucial and complex during crisis because of this increased tension. To the extent that, sometimes, glances or movements of others may condition board activity and discussions. An independent director provides a colorful example: 'At times the most important actor is not easy to identify. There are times when you really do not understand what is happening but you have to look at the glances, see who the chairperson is looking at, or what member X is doing or saying, because he/she may be just an independent director, but one with a notable influence on the dominant shareholder or the chairperson.'

The outcome

The last element to discuss in this chapter is the outcome of the decision-making process. We have identified in our research three major outcomes of decision-making under crisis in light of this description of board processes: delay, inadequate resolution or resolution.

Following the logic presented across this chapter, the most probable outcome is delay in decision-making. Indeed, longer decision-making processes are most likely: more abundant and more complex problems, increased demands of information for problem-solving, increased asymmetry of goals, more participation and debate plus increased tension, end up for sure in a delayed decision-making process. The process we described thus far pushes to turn the process longer, leading to procrastination (and even to eventual abortion) of the decision.

Delay can also be a symbolic strategy of the board to abort or reject decision-making. In the words of a former chairperson of a large technology company, still as independent director with several boards: 'Things are never rejected. They are accepted or they are postponed. The elegant form of rejecting a project is postponing it. This is the educated form of killing something.' A seasoned CEO agrees: 'Boards are often there to say no without saying so.'

Inadequacy of the solution is the second type of outcome. If there is no decision deferral, due to executives' effort not to postpone decisions because of immediate performance implications for themselves, there are for sure higher odds for mistake, leading to decision by oversight (Cohen, March and Olsen, 1972). In other words, there is a higher risk of mistake when the decision-making process is not postponed; there are more decisions to take in less or the same time, so there is less thinking or more board workload, thus larger risk of mistakes. When there is no more actual work dedication (for instance, because the boards are already too busy), the speed of decision falters and delay is inevitable.

Survival (or at least, very critical) decisions are more frequent under crisis. In the case of survival decisions, the situation has to move fast and, thus, it is easier to decide by oversight. An independent director in the media industry explains: 'Decisions on survival accelerate, even if it is not always easy during crisis to discern which ones are related to survival from those which are on growth.'

There are other factors contended earlier (such as ownership structure, power of the executives or company size) that influence final decision-making speed and, hence, the flow of solutions. In the words of a CEO of a large listed company: 'In large organizations with no dominant block-holding, the executive team acts as the real owner.' Company size may inversely relate to decision-making speed, because when a company is small they can (and have to) run faster to survive. A director in the private capital industry endorses this perspective: 'Crisis is much worse for small companies. Because large companies have the inertia that smaller companies do not have. This means that you [small firms] could fall into the red ink very easily and need to restructure.' Conversely, larger firms may be trapped by this inertia and this (inertia) may backfire if the problem-solving search of other firms facing similar problems leads to superior solutions; this is indeed the nature of threat-rigidity effect (Ocasio, 1995).

The paradox is that this timely connection between actors, issues, choices and solutions may lead to final decisions, not necessarily in the name of rigor, but only as a consequence of this temporary encounter. This is a classical trait of the garbage-can model of choice (Cohen, March and Olsen, 1972). An independent director provides support to this assertion: 'When deciding a strategic acquisition to expand elsewhere, one may think this follows careful analysis. But this is not necessarily so. Decision may be influenced by those who drop on the table the first name for a target. Once making an acquisition is approved, this is often more important than careful analysis of potential targets.'

As described earlier, decision by resolution is less likely because of forces pushing towards delay. It has been long contended (Trull, 1966) that decision success is not only contingent on decision accuracy, but on this effective decision accuracy enforced through skillful management of implementation. More recent literature (Bourgeois and Eisenhardt, 1988; Baum and Wally, 2003) suggests that fast strategic decision-making predicts some measures of performance such as firm growth and profit. Therefore, we can conclude that success of decision is contingent on time.

In other cases, there is actual decision by resolution but for the wrong reasons, another classical random outcome of garbage-can decision-making (Cohen, March and Olsen, 1972). An executive director provides an excellent example of this logic:

> There was a situation in which we needed funding for a new project. The board finally voted for the option of issuing bonds; instead of other more traditional type of funding (e.g. bank). The

underlying intention—in fact, not well hidden by some directors— was to have someone else saying no (to the project). Because if you issue debt, you need to have a rating and logically there are more external scrutiny requirements. So the hidden interest -for some- was basically to kill the project, not to assume any further risk. In turn, it was successful for the absolutely wrong reasons: our debt was issued and it was well received by the market, while bank funding became eventually tougher and more expensive due to growing credit scarcity.

Ultimately, as we have already argued in this chapter, there are other organizational results of this decision-making process regardless of the decision outcome. Decisions and the way they are made may hinder effectiveness in the executive team and fall downstream in the organization. There are, in principle, two main costs resulting from this situation.

The first is the emotional erosion for the executive team, as in more pressure, more difficult decisions to be made, increased workload, preparation and discussion. A CEO in a large global firm gives a view of this: 'The frequency of meetings, at least here, has not changed. But duration is longer. Meetings are longer, with more debate, problems are damned more complex.' This has an effect by spiraling through executive motivation, thus creating tension or 'checkout', especially in those closer to the CEO or executive directors. In principle, less unanimity might erode management motivation. Postponement of decisions may also cause frustration and anger for executives and top management, as threats to personal sense of control lead to psychological reactance (Erez and Kanfer, 1983). Eventually, all this should be factored in as part of the actual quality and cost of decision under crisis.

The second component of cost (indeed a potential risk) is the overall effect of this process on implementation ability.

Less unanimity of opinions and decisions in the boardroom might generate tension and influence executive motivation. Thus, this has likely implications in implementation, such as decreased energy and less unity of action. The chairperson in a private technology firm agrees: 'The discussion and lack of unanimity play this way. And executives see there is no unity. This demotivates them, besides the fact that it is more difficult to push things that are not widely accepted.'

This description of the board dynamics is consistent with a skeptical view of decisions in the boardroom during crisis. Decisions are delayed or, if not, decision quality is decreased. This is, broadly speaking, consistent with the garbage-can model of choice (Cohen, March and Olsen, 1972) holding that uncertainty and ambiguity may lead to changing decision priorities rather than paralysis. Our interviewees reveal that decision by resolution is not the most expected outcome of decision-making under crisis, and that symbolic rather than substantial decisions are the fastest to be made. By adding this conclusion to the behavioral dynamics among the different typologies of directors on the board—parochial interest in safeguarding individual privilege, centralization of decision by CEOs/chairpersons, strain to survival rather than stimuli to participate for independent directors, and more risk averse choices for everyone—we end up with a rather cynical conclusion on the way that boards function under crisis. Of course, we are aware that this is an extreme picture and that plenty of boards work in the most appropriate manner to face the crisis as effectively as possible. However, we cannot ignore that the image coming from our sample of board members gives us a much less reassuring representation of what boardroom decision-making during crisis might be (and, perhaps, not only under crisis).

6
Board Activity as Routines

In this chapter we aim to provide a view of organizational settings that shares similar decision characteristics to those of boards. This might be helpful for investigating the relevance of management cognition in decision-making. We address the issue of cognition through the concept of routines and their relevance for understanding decision-making processes. Another crucial issue we explore here is attention, leading to awareness of crisis itself. In the current economic crisis, only when decision makers became aware that this crisis situation was 'nonstandard', that is, a situation where existing organizational routines failed to confront crisis, did they enter into a more innovative search mode. Not surprisingly, boardrooms tried initially to apply traditional recipes as the standard operating procedures at the outset of crisis. It was a long time before many at the organizational apex (and the majority of external observers) noticed that the nature of crisis was dissimilar to other previous recession situations—and realized that this was probably the most intense in nature after the Great Depression.

After all, there is no crisis without awareness, as, borrowing an example from the highly demanding practice of surgical medicine, the first key to avoid medical accidents is to recognize that something is wrong (Gaba, Maxwell and DeAnda, 1987). Also in this chapter, we will compare decision-making for boards during crisis with decision-making for other critical decision-making groups. Notably other groups with central responsibilities in their organizations—such as firefighters, airline crew and surgical or military teams—have often been related to high reliability demands (Weick, Sutcliffe and Obstfeld, 1999). In a way, a top management team or board of directors should be also targeted as a high reliability environment, in the sense that their decisions and actions could, in theory, be highly consequential for the objectives of their stakeholders, or for their very own organizational existence.

We believe this is an interesting comparison as there has been a significant amount of folklore about the boardroom as a 'black box' of directors and CEOs, and this comparison with other critical workforces should help shed some light on a crucial question when exploring boards: are top managers so different from the rest of mankind when making decisions in difficult situations? We believe that a reply to this question is instrumental in order to extract some learning to be applied to the boardroom realm during crisis.

One of the critical assets for managers is 'attention' towards their environment. Nothing really happens unless something is noticed, understood and then acted upon. Crisis might have prompted this attention. Reaction to the environment might be activated by organizational routines (for an updated and in-depth review of the literature on management routines, see Becker, 2004), or rules of appropriateness when it comes to other nonstandard problem-solving situations.

We save cognition efforts by applying preconfigured scripts: in a way, this means to create or re-create activities ('routines') in order to reduce the amount of time, energy and, ultimately, cognition to be devoted to resolving main daily activities. When we speak about routines, we refer to an organizational phenomenon; routines often are reflected on at the individual level ('habits'). For example, most of us do not enter into a problem-solving mode in order to perform our basic tasks at the office; we behave and act as we deem appropriate, according to our identities, and we use standard procedures or processes ('routines') to do so. Likewise, as individuals we do not enter into problem-solving mode to select our attire for the office, to select a driving route from work back home or to face daily personal cleaning activities. We have built across time standardized habits for these things.

Conversely, we apply rules of appropriateness when existing preconfigured routines are unable to solve the immediate issue and decision makers opt to 'satisfice' when facing 'unprogrammed' decision-making situations. This means (and this is truly relevant for problem-solving and decision-making during crisis) that organizations seldom look for optimizing solutions, but rather 'escape' from the search of optimal solutions and feel satisfied with 'good enough' solutions.

The nature of routines and their importance for boardroom decision-making

Most individual decisions are made in organizational settings, that is, in the work environment, in family, in churches, in political parties or at any other type of social situation. Therefore, if the rational decision-making model does not fully fit facts, we still need a model of decision-making to be able to understand firm behavior and organizational action.

The notion of bounded rationality was developed by March and Simon (1958) for organizational settings in order to address this issue. Rules of appropriateness and organizational routines are driven by bounded rationality. We suggest that something similar happens in the boardroom. The use of rules of appropriateness in boardroom decision-making has been already suggested by several scholars (Ocasio, 1999; Davidson *et al.*, 2002). Within this assumption of bounded rationality, organizations operate by dividing large problems into subsets of more manageable issues in order to make them easier to be solved by individuals. Simultaneously, this turns many organizational activities into routine. Large, complex organizations would probably be unfeasible without large amounts of routine. Not surprisingly, it has been suggested that routines occupy 'the crucial nexus between structure and action, between the organization as an object and organizing as a process' (Pentland and Rueter, 1994), a crucial point that we shall come back to later in this chapter.

Establishing routine means that tasks can be performed smoothly (Rumelt, 1995). In other words, and from an information-processing perspective, this means that routines economize on cognition (Bromiley, 2005). People in an organization do not need to invent how to react in front of most events that the organization regularly faces. In organizational settings, we have a great deal of routines helping us (as organizational actors and the organization as a group) to react to most events.

In most management literature, the term 'routine' seems to refer to recurring collective (interaction) patterns. These routines might be unobservable (for example, mental patterns) or observable (as in habits or routines, depending if they are individual or collective). These are fundamentally patterns of interaction and, thus, collective in nature. We are talking about organizational routines, even though individual habits could be—and very often are—a crucial component of these organizational routines. Borrowing an example from a deep crisis situation, Karl Weick's study of the Tenerife air disaster showed that the relationship between organizational routines and individual behaviors may be crucial to reach organizational goals and can be dislocated (and end up in massive organizational failure) when individuals behave 'in a manner that is more individual than collective' (Weick, 1990).

To be clear, routine does not necessarily mean simple or non-specific. Routines can be precise templates for action, describing clear operating procedures in almost any conceivable circumstance. Organizations have been able across time to typify and establish 'standard' scripts for very complex situations, thus turning them into routine. Bromiley (2005) suggests a nice example that illustrates this complexity: there are often organizational routines (meta-routines) modifying other routines, for instance total quality management (TQM) procedures in industrial settings or procedures to change core curricula in schools.

Routines may be idiosyncratic for a given organization and there may be also institutionalized common routines. For example, the structured analysis of any given investment opportunity is commonplace across mostly any firm and there are similar routines driving this process everywhere (such as estimating future cash outflows and inflows, using a set of investment selection criteria—NPV, IRR, Pay Back—or defining a hurdle cost rate for discounting cash-flow streams). All that can be labeled routine. Another key characteristic of routines is that they are repetitive (Cohen *et al.*, 1996; Winter, 1990). Routines get to be so after successful repetition, as they provide good enough and stable solutions (Amit and Belcourt, 1999; Oliver, 1992) and, eventually, provide predictability (Cyert and March, 1963; Nelson and Winter, 1982; Feldman, 2003).

Routines are also a recognized source of inertia (Hannan and Freeman, 1984). They may lead to inertia due to the investment (sunk costs) incurred to create the routine (Becker, 2004). Paradoxically, routines have been also conceptualized as a source of change (Feldman and Pentland, 2003; Feldman, 2003). For example, Gersick and Hackman (1990) suggested that large enough external shocks might (or should) overrule routines by offsetting the benefits of cognitive efficiency ('inertia') provided by existing routines. Routines have been also proved important in organizational adaptation (Feldman, 2003; Feldman and Rafaeli, 2002; Pentland and Rueter, 1994; Pentland, 1995). This line of thought is particularly appealing when analyzing top management teams' reactions to crisis: crisis might have had an effect on the nature of some existing routines and its (crisis) intensity and length may have been related to the adaptability of those prevailing routines to the demands of the new situation. However, despite this impressive array of theory, the notion of routines is still far from univocal in the literature, and contemporary understanding of the concept remains still imprecise (Jones and Craven, 2001).

Why routines are relevant for exploration at in the boardroom?

Time pressure seems to increase the likelihood of routine choices despite inadequacy of selection. Previous knowledge has a strong impact in choice in a situation of time pressure and risk, ignoring relevant information or new evidence in the decision-making process (Betsch *et al.*, 1999; Betsch *et al.*, 2001). In terms of crisis, a consideration of routine is relevant despite the cyclical nature of crisis, by definition, a non-routine event. However, time pressure might be pushing boards towards the use of routinized solutions.

The proliferation of repeated routines might be, at least partially, behind some ineffective behaviors of executive decision-making during crisis. As we suggested earlier, a change in the routines of boards during crisis might have helped boards tackle crisis more effectively. At the same time, repeated routines may go against change and adaptation, which might be counterproductive for reacting properly to the environment during crisis. We believe that boards have primarily used existing scripts of behavior, at least in the initial stages of crisis management, such as using pre-learned routines—for instance, those related to cost management—that come from experience in previous downturns.

This initial behavior might have worsened effects (as in attacking symptoms rather than causes) in the current crisis, which has turned out to be eventually deeper and longer than expected. There are other indications that problem-solving during the current crisis is basically grounded on existing routines. For example, the lack in many organizations of specific protocols to manage exceptional crises affecting all stakeholders (Pearson and Mitroff, 1993; Alpasian, Green and Mitroff, 2009), and the relative stability of board composition across time (at least, in the sample for our research) during this long crisis and the (apparent) slow reaction of boards are, in our view, indications of inertia in decision-making.

While we mentioned before that routines may often anticipate what needs to be done in any given situation, other routines may allow far greater leeway in their interpretation, for example those associated with senior management (Coombs and Metcalfe, 2000). This is, we think, a relevant point for the assessment of boardroom reaction during crisis. As we have argued in the previous chapters, there were probably not enough routines or templates associated with the reaction to crisis, which made the reaction towards crisis less effective (or more untimely and costly) in terms of decision-making. This less structured (routinized) behavior is conceptually closer to that of an organized anarchy with high degrees of uncertainty (Perrow, 1994).

If rule-based behavior in the boardroom has not been effective enough to tackle crisis, and seems to push the organizational apex (board) towards organized anarchy, is there any learning we can apply to the boardroom from other decision-making groups under pressure? This is the question we shall explore next.

Are boards of directors and other (critical) decision-making groups so different?

As mentioned in the introduction to this chapter, a point we deem important here is the comparison between decision-making in the boardroom and that of other critical decision-making groups. As crisis is the specific context of our exploration, we are including here for comparison other decision-making groups in critical situations, namely situations we could label as 'life or death' or, at least, highly consequential both for decision makers and for those who these decisions might affect. Within this category, we have included reviews from accounts about a number of critical workgroups such as air crews, surgical teams, military teams or firefighters and multimember judges, all pertaining to groups with high reliability demands. Our purpose here is not performing an in-depth comparison among all these groups (this would exceed our goal[1]), but grounding some conclusions on differences (and particularly common issues) that could enlighten our portrait of boards during crisis.

While traditional literature on the topic has labeled high reliability organizations (HROs) as adaptive forms for an increasingly complex environment (Weick, Sutcliffe and Obstfeld, 1999), this need of high reliability is increasingly not limited to organizations and settings that are typically complex or particularly demanding (for example, nuclear power-generation plants, naval aircraft carriers, air traffic control systems) but also to mainstream organizations. Thus, we shall try to connect the main common issues between these decision-making groups and board members during crisis, in order to extract some significance of transversal application for boardrooms.

It has been suggested that potentially devastating catastrophes might be the result of a number of separate small events that become connected and amplified in non-predictable and inexplicable ways (Weick, 1990; Perrow, 1994). This seems to have been the case for large accidents in the air-traffic control space, the chemical industry and others (see for example Weick, 1988; 1990; Vaughan, 1996). While this might not be an immediate comparison for boardroom decision-making during crisis, we believe our analysis can benefit from it.

Through analysis of incidents and accidents in several spaces a number of common issues in these major crisis events have been found. We believe these lessons are fundamental to enrich the research of boards during crisis as they are related to: (a)

---

[1] For an in-depth view of recent literature on risk, reliability and safety see for example Leveson *et al.*, 2009 and Gephart, Van Maanen and Oberlechner, 2009.

effective communication during crisis, (b) healthy exertion of hierarchical or formal authority, (c) balanced team composition and abilities fostering effective coordination and surveillance (to match environmental demands) and (d) preservation of meaningfulness of roles, particularly in temporary organizations, which is often the case for many critical mission groups— projects, missions, flights—but frequently also for many boardroom situations and teams.

Effective communication: assumptions and misunderstandings are the worst enemies of knowledge

Effective communication has been reported as vital to reach high reliability in organizations (Roberts and Bea, 2001). In any crisis situation, there is a high probability that 'false hypotheses will develop and persist' (Weick, 1990). This seems something to be avoided. Thus, candid and non-ambiguous communication is crucial in these critical environment settings. Weick's (1990) advice is that if things do not make sense, speak up (sooner rather than later), as there is evidence suggesting that the amount of conversation exchange and performance reliability co-vary in very trying environments (La Porte and Consolini, 1991) and that nonstop talk, both verbal and nonverbal, is a crucial foundation for coordination-driven disasters in complex systems (Eisenhardt, 1992).

If there is an activity in which organizational rules and routines are particularly relevant this is air traffic, notably in all activities related to control systems, due to the complexity and demand from the environment (Weick, Sutcliffe and Obstfeld, 1999); nuclear generation plants and space shuttles are also highly routinized activities: the same is also true of military missions. Issues of communication are reported to have been central in critical accidents in those spaces (Weick, 1990; Snook, 2000).

This effectiveness of communication is particularly difficult to attain in connection to inevitable reductions of attention (due, for instance, to stress produced during crisis). Stress is a significant factor affecting judgment in critical situations (Holroyd and Lazarus, 1982) and it has long been known that best performance is reached under average levels of pressure. It is inevitable, therefore, that stress heavily influences a team's performance during crisis.

Another hurdle to effective communication during crisis is related to social constraints and individual assumptions. When analyzing a friendly fire shoot-down incident, for example, Snook (2000) describes a related example associated partially with pluralistic ignorance, a phenomenon that prevents people from questioning misunderstandings or disagreements about an issue, due in large part to social constrictions. Something analogous has been reported in other high reliability environments such as nuclear plants (Sheridan, 1981). Pluralistic ignorance has been also reported in corporate boardroom settings (Westphal and Bednar, 2005) and it may be a significant obstacle to frank communication, particularly during crisis. This point is particularly relevant in relation to redundancy, typical in environments with high reliability requirements: if divergences are not voiced, redundancy of actors may backfire. We will look more at this in the next section.

Finally, effective communication often entails something of a challenge: ambiguous language in hierarchical communication might have been at the heart of some catastrophes, particularly in times of stress (Weick, 1990). Whether it is in the cockpit, during a military mission planning meeting or in the boardroom (particularly during crisis situations), when (and where) there is a marked hierarchy it is likely that creating equal communication becomes a difficult if not impossible task, and that these attempts end up turning into upward and downward (hierarchical) communication, with the increased risk of some pieces of information critical for achieving organizational goals being lost.

Pigs looking at watches: effective exertion of power

There is a lot of stress in the boardroom during crisis. Stress, as we mentioned before, is a lever for mistakes: it 'paves the way for its own intensification' (Weick, 1990). Stress increases complexity of issues (for example, by increasing errors) and reduces slack ('tightens coupling'), thus increasing threat. As already mentioned in previous chapters, threat to organizations frequently leads to centralization (Staw, Sandelands and Dutton, 1981).

Due to decision centralization, the increasing tight coupling between role (or hierarchy, or any form of authority) and solution may lead to poor decision or even disaster. Ineffectiveness of this type has been named a factor in several large accidents and incidents of this sort (Vaughan, 1996). A comparable phenomenon (intensified centralization and increased exertion of formal power) might have happened in the boardroom during crisis, with the decision-effectiveness outcomes that we discussed in Chapter 4.

Indeed, boardroom hierarchical authority or risk aversion might have been causal to increase the amount of decisions to be queued at the board (not necessarily taken, as discussed in the previous chapter). Evidence from other settings seems to suggest that, in order to seek reliability, decisions should be made at the lower organizational levels, with the correct and relevant information (Roberts, Stout and Halpern, 1994; La Porte and Consolini, 1991), both for a matter of quality of information and timeliness. The latter is particularly important under crisis or in a hazard situation.

'Pigs looking at watches' is the expression that a senior military officer uses to describe his own feelings in front of a situation he is not able to decipher (Snook, 2000). Consistently, specific knowledge (or lack thereof) of board members about issues of the business they run might have been central to boardroom and business performance during crisis (Davies, 2010).

The attitude of leadership towards their own exertion of power (particularly when there is a strong hierarchical relationship) is also vital, as it may avoid or promote fact-finding and hinder or foster effective communication. Hubris or social face-saving might turn things worse until it is too late, particularly on critical activities. This quite often seems to be the case in disasters (see for example, Weick, 1990; 2007); as there is difficulty in being really challenging in front of someone with strong formal (or even informal) influence.

Thus, the ability and attitude of the chairperson or CEO (or any other powerful director in the boardroom) to receive input and reflect might establish the difference between 'good' or 'bad' decisions. A monolithic exertion of power may lead to other perverse and non-intended consequences such as herding or groupthink, and eventually poor quality of decision. That view of 'decentralization and empowerment' (Roberts, Stout and Halpern, 1994) in these critical environments seems to be most effective when time is of the essence and technical competence at the point of decision affects the outcome of choice (e.g. in the operation of aircraft carriers). Not surprisingly, networked groups have proven superior—faster and more accurate in decision-making—to purely hierarchical groups in crisis-related settings (Schraagen, Huis in 't Veld and de Koning, 2010).

So, redundancy seems to emerge as a main determinant to improve decision-making effectiveness. Redundancy has been praised in high reliability environments. However, redundancy may lead to the opposite outcome: no one making sure of the issues out of overreliance on the other. A redundant structure might be beneficial, but it has an obscure side (Weick, 2001) because redundancy may encourage diffusion of responsibility. This risk (overreliance out of redundancy) might be also tangible for the roles of chairperson and CEO, in companies in which those are separate roles. In fact, unity of action is indeed the main argument for duality in boards (Finkelstein and D'Aveni, 1994), against the most extended view in main contemporary Corporate Governance codes of separation of the CEO and chairperson roles.

Selecting, developing and leveraging crucial skills to respond to high reliability demands

The continuous and effective integration of processes and collective mindfulness has been labeled as a crucial resource to create stronger systems (Weick and Roberts, 1993; Weick, Sutcliffe and Obstfeld, 1999). To achieve that reliability, there is a need to enroll the right people with the right social interaction. Something analogous should happen in the boardroom. Crisis-induced stress influences during periods of regression (Weick, 1990), thus embedding checks and balances in the system often through social interaction is essential (Weick and Roberts, 1993). From that perspective, composition and interaction within a board team are key components to achieve success.

Selection of individuals is crucial to achieve high reliability, something fully related with board composition. In these highly demanding environments, it is not only technical expertise that matters, but also individual interpersonal skills, because of the need to maintain effective communication and real reliance on collective mindfulness. Borrowing an example from the legal system of justice, there is some reason to believe that decisions reached by multimember courts may be more accurate—that is, it is more likely they would be viewed as correct by the relevant community than those reached by a single-judge court (Quinn, 2012).

At the same time, building this diversity may have other effects. Revesz (1997) found in D.C. Circuit cases involving challenges to Environmental Protection Agency (EPA) rulings that: 'a Democrat sitting with two Republicans votes more conservatively than a Republican sitting with two Democrats' (Revesz, 1997; Quinn, 2012). There are two different forces at work here; ideologically extreme members of the judging panel will often have a greater incentive to collect costly information than would their (more) moderate colleagues. For example, it has been suggested that ideologically motivated behavior might actually give rise to greater exchange of information and better deliberation (Spitzer and Talley, 2011). However, Epstein *et al.* (2011) suggest that the threat of imposing costs on colleagues by writing a dissenting article may be enough to cause (at least) one of the judges in the majority to moderate his or her views.

There are a number of potential explanations for those effects. One conceivable explanation lies on the consequences of panel diversity on information-processing and debate. A group with dissenting views (for example, a group composed of judges with very different mindsets or backgrounds) might evaluate a wider range of perspectives when deliberating than another group with common (or very similar) views. This balance in the background of members is an interesting learning point for the boardroom, conceptually connected with the traditional upper echelons' school of thought (Hambrick and Mason, 1984) and with potential applications to the diversity composition of the boardroom.

Another possible explanation is the potential for a minority (or lonely) judge on a group to act as a whistleblower (Cross and Tiller, 1998). There are theoretical benefits for this dissenter, such as the possibility to influence law via rehearing or reconsideration by a superior court, or strengthening personal reputation. A comparable situation might be the case of an isolated non-executive director voicing his or her concerns in order to influence the board decision, or the converse pattern, when an independent external director could be affected ('abducted') by the load of social influence and not voice high enough (valid) concerns due to issues of potential social punishment and internal political risk.

These results show that individual views and group composition both have significant effects on an individual's choice, but that the views of others are an even better predictor of an individual's decision than our own views (Quinn, 2012). We are, despite our own ideologies and views, significantly affected by the ideas of others. We decide in social settings (March and Simon, 1958; Simon, 1961), seldom isolated from others, so social influence is crucial. Not surprisingly, risk of cognitive biases (such as herding) seems higher during crisis, particularly if there is a clear dominant role in the boardroom that is able to influence the group. We have already argued in previous chapters that patterns for boardroom reporting change during crisis, affecting dynamics of decision-making and potentially quality and timeliness of decision.

Highly reliable organizations have been characterized by three different attributes (Roberts and Bea, 2001): (a) these organizations try to learn as much as possible and relentlessly pursue to know what they don't know, (b) incentive systems for these organizations aim to recognize costs (of failure) as well as the benefits of reliability, and (c) these organizations try to communicate the big picture to everyone around, and they also try to keep everyone involved in how they fit within it. These three traits are related to a number of crucial activities in the boardroom, namely evaluation, training, composition renewal and internal communication. A significant point is the need for an evergreen alignment between both board composition and dynamics and the demands from the environment. Despite this need, inertia might have turned the board more stable than is required: in other words, not enough—or slow—changes in routines and/or in their internal composition to effectively tackle crisis.

If you are not the organization man, who are you?

There are issues of identity and structure in decision-making behavior during crisis. After all, and this applies equally in the boardroom, rules of appropriateness are intrinsically related to identity (Ocasio, 1999). When a situation of extreme crisis destroys the sense of identity and organizational belonging of individuals, then the cohesion of the organization is more problematic, or even unfeasible (Weick, 1993; 1996) and performance may be seriously affected (and the very existence of the organization might be at risk).

Sometimes during crisis, an organization may lose its sense of identity. In Weick's (1996) words: 'When a formal structure collapses, there are no leaders, roles or routines; the situation no longer makes sense.' This breech of identity turns out to be critical for the 'organization man'. When all the former collapses, we are on our own. In other words, highly reliable structures are resilient sources of collective sense-making (Weick, 1996).

Thus, the final point of this comparison between decision-making environments is related to the consistency between the individual and group responses during crisis; because under some extreme circumstances, all frames of reference for organizational actors disappear. Is there such a thing as coordinated decision-making without coordinated activity?

A significant point here is the connection between structure and structuring. The structure—as organizational framework—talks about positions, rules, procedures and authority (Ranson, Hinings and Greenwood, 1980; Weick, 2001) but that does not help us to explicate the loss of connection among organizational members in the case of major crisis. At the same time, structuring is related to the pattern of social interactions that shape and are shaped by the organizational framework. It is precisely the latter that helps us to explain more properly the loss of connection among organizational members that can happen during major crisis.

This process of organizing (Weick, 2001; Ranson, Hinings and Greenwood, 1980) is related to three different aspects: (1) interpretive schemes or taken-for-granted frames constituting purposive values or interests within the organization (what Ranson, Hinings and Greenwood label as provinces of meaning), (2) dependencies of power settling (and unifying) potential separations between alternative interpretive schemes and (3) contextual constraints within the conditions of the environment (Pfeffer and Salancik, 1978) or the accommodation to external demands to the organization (Lawrence and Lorsch, 1967).

This loss of frames of reference (Conner, 1992) seems to have been relevant in the case of several catastrophic events in high reliability demand environments (Weick, 1990; 1996). The mutation of an organizational group into a collection of separate individuals with their own peculiar ways of reacting—whether it is by failure in their interaction process; by their inability to effectively form a group; or by their transformation, because of stress, into a horde of disengaged individuals—might have extremely detrimental effects in group performance (Weick, 1990; Lazarus and Folkman, 1984).

The failure in integrating these components in the organizing process has been reported to give birth to large organizational disasters (Weick, 1990; 1996; 2001). Preserving these components in the structuring process provides group resilience in the face of organizational crisis.

In the context of the board, the ability to maintain common interpretive schemes and shared purpose in the face of crisis helps create 'teamness' in the boardroom even if, as discussed earlier, crisis is a social phenomenon and, therefore, narratives about crisis differ, often even within the same boardroom. Not surprisingly, the creation and maintenance of a common culture, or the development and preservation of a body of common values, might help organizational forms, including the board, to pursue higher reliability (Weick and Roberts, 1993; Weick, 1987).

We believe that this loss of common ground in organizational crises, and the subsequent impact on group performance, is more likely in the board realm than in more structured, steady organizational forms. This is because many forms in which boards are organized—such as the board of directors, but particularly other fluid committees within the board—are often temporary forms and/or their frequency of shared work is usually sparse. Something similar applies to board teams with a short tenure together and, thus, at initial stages of their history (in other words, with weaker links among members). We have to consider, however, the strength of the boardroom institutional environment as a countervailing mechanism to compensate for potential losses of reference in the boardroom due to the frequent and numerous ties among actors in these interlocked settings (Granovetter, 1985; Mizruchi, 1996).

What can we learn from all this that can be used in the boardroom? Cyert and March (1963) assumed that search within organizations is mainly stimulated by a certain problem: the existence of a problem is the engine that drives innovation. Given organizational limitations of rationality, there is not an 'objective function' to be optimized, but a certain level of aspirations to be satisfied (Simon, 1957). These aspiration levels are often framed by previous performance, past history or comparison (something more problematic in the face of a crisis). This is not different in most decision-making groups. However, when organizations cannot use a preconfigured set of routines to answer to unexpected events, then we enter into problem-solving mode, and structure and routines become less useful which is, in a way, what is more easily promoted during crisis.

No matter how loosely coupled a system is, it is susceptible to become tighter and more complex when there is overload, misperception, regression and individualized response (Weick, 1990). The same applies for boards: even otherwise inconsequential changes—(such as market changes) fostered by issues such as communication, leadership and hierarchies, internal coordination of skills or the resilience of the organizational system—can tighten couplings and foster complexity in crisis in almost any organizational setting. This is, we argue, what pushes the boardroom towards a less routinized type of activity during crisis. Random plays also a key role in decision-making. But it is obviously not easy to admit, particularly for practitioners, that random might be so important in regular practice.

chapter 7

Moving Forward: Do Boards Need to Improve their Decision-Making during Crisis, and How?

In a recent film (*Margin Call,* 2011) Jeremy Irons—fictional bank CEO John Tuld—tells a younger banker to explain issues to him as he would 'to a young child or a Golden Retriever, in plain English; as it was not brains that got him there'.

This is just an amusing illustration of the phenomenon, but interest in executives has become common currency everywhere. In many places in the world senior managers and entrepreneurs are becoming, or have become, well-known stars comparable to actors, elite sportsmen/women or top politicians. This fact is not completely new: there are older examples such as Howard Hughes, Henry Ford or Aristotle Onassis as well as more recent ones such as Larry Ellison, Richard Branson or the late Steve Jobs. Some sort of that leadership romance (Meindl, Ehrlich and Dukerich, 1985) we mention in the beginning of this book is in the air, which has put senior managers and other businessmen under growing public scrutiny. Managers are considered supermen or wonder women but, as in the humoristic movie scene in the opening of this section, they are just regular human beings, with significant levels of responsibility and power, facing very complex crisis-related issues.

A central intention of this book has been to offer a crisp, close portrait of the effects of crisis on boardroom decision-making processes as seen through the eyes of insiders. By building a credible practitioner-oriented but theoretically relevant narrative of boards we have dug extensively into the perception of crisis in boardroom settings and in organizational decision-making approaches. Although these approaches are far from economically rational-minded approaches to TMT decision-making, we think they better capture the nuances of boardroom contemporary decision-making during crisis.

Surprisingly our sources, rather than putting the emphasis on themselves as enlightened business men/women, show a significantly skeptical view of decision-making at the board level. Our role in this book is not that of being sympathetic to this skepticism, although our personal experience may lead us to agree with many of the interviewees' opinions. Rather, our task is to interpret the evidence. We found that this skepticism rises out of the prevalence and, to a certain extent, dominance of three factors in boards' decision-making: short-termism, centralization and parochialism. These factors come from the interpretation of the interviews and supporting literature. We used organizational theory to take a closer look at these factors: in particular, we used the garbage-can model of choice to look at the role played by parochialism and self-interest in the decision-making process at board level.

We argue that board decisions are too short-term oriented and this keeps reproducing key issues, which in recent years has led to the current economic crisis. Our research also argues the need to compensate for the effect of short-term performance focus and market signaling (obviously the latter being more significant for listed public firms who need to stick closely to their earnings guidance) on corporate governance behaviors during this crisis. In other words, more balance between short- and long-term objectives seems to be required, particularly for organizations to grow any stronger after this current crisis.

Despite short-termism, boards are putting their hands on as many decisions as possible. Centralization is mainly driven by risk aversion, since centralized decisions are the other side of the coin of boards with lower trust of managers and organizational structures below them during crisis. The research outcome calls for the need to continuously define the fit of board composition and board access and exit mechanisms for directors. It is needed to maintain a strong level of professional independence in board judgment, which is considered crucial in the face of external crisis. By centralizing decisions, boards are affecting decision-making processes and turning them into very complex and analytical ones. Complexity of decision-making, and the growing amount of decisions, make decision-making slower and uneasy.

However, pace and difficulty of decisions also depends on the higher degree of self-interest that crisis-driven uncertainty puts on boards. The final decisional outcomes are delay and postponement—as our main theoretical inspiration for this book, the perspective of the garbage-can model of choice, would have suggested about the prevalence of flight and oversight choices. Not without irony, our interviews show that board decision-making process during crisis looks similar to that of the organized anarchies provocatively described by James March and colleagues for universities and military organizations. We could not have found a result that is further from the taken-for-granted view mainly spread by business media and public opinion about the economically rational board members. We acknowledge that our findings challenge the idea that board monitoring of management during crisis is being completely effective, or even helping firms get out of crisis any faster. On the contrary, our exploration seems to suggest that, specifically because of boardroom internal processes during crisis, decision-making quality might be at risk.

Despite differences of practices among different countries (for a comparative review of different national corporate governance models see Aguilera and Jackson, 2003, 2010), board members' independence seems the main value to preserve and the logic is, in principle, applicable to other settings: rigor in access (for example, independent selection of directors) and rigorous performance management of boards (such as impartial external assessment of the board team both at the individual and group levels) are key during crisis. Maintaining this discipline may help organizations to prevent future crises and be more resilient in the face of impending negative events.

In sum, some of the elements of boardroom decision-making processes already present in the past are still shaping board decision-making under crisis. In fact, we believe that parochialism, centralization and short-termism were already present in board decision-making before crisis.

However, having these elements favored the diffusion of current crisis. We, as well as public opinion at wide, would have expected short-termism, centralization and parochialism to have a lower impact on board decision-making as part of their effort to overcome crisis. Interestingly, despite crisis or, perhaps, because of it, the opinion of our interviewees is that these elements are now more strongly affecting board decision-making. This means that effective learning has not yet taken place at boardroom decision-making level. Perhaps the current crisis is too recent to generate visible traces of learning; however, it is counterintuitive evidence that crises have thus far accentuated elements that are supposed to be related to crisis development (when not to its causality).

In the following section we outline the managerial implications of the key arguments derived from our sources, describing a few initiatives that could address the critical issues raised in the previous chapters.

Managerial implications

In this book we not only aim to contribute to the description of the effects of crisis on the decision-making at board level; we also have the humble ambition to provide some suggestions to practitioners for removing (or lessening) some of the critical issues we have detected in the crisis-functioning of boards of directors. We believe this attempt is crucially important at this stage; it would be wrong not to speak our mind on how to improve board decision-making processes after having investigated them. This is particularly important given our attention to the growing skepticism and dismay emerging from our interviewees' accounts.

Grounded on the previous accounts and evidence derived from the interpretation of the interviews, in this section we try to put together a number of potential suggestions for practitioners. We identify six main areas of managerial implications: (1) early assessment and reaction to crisis, (2) balancing board composition, (3) maintaining or improving the strategy process, (4) helping change the CEO role, (5) developing new internal board routines and (6) other—like those related to compensation and the institutional environment.

Rather than universally valid and generally applicable recommendations, in each of these areas of implications we aim at developing normative arguments that may serve as points of reflection for practitioners and potential areas of further investigations for researchers. We hope that our normative effort may prove helpful for executives in boardroom positions in order to better recognize their current challenges and more effectively tackle crisis. In Table 7.1 we summarize the areas of implications and some of the normative indications we derive from our research in this book.

TABLE 7.1 Main domains of prescriptions for boardrooms during crisis

Area of prescription	Main themes
Early assessment of crisis and timely reaction	• (Strategic) risk management frameworks and systems • Protocols of crisis reaction
Balancing composition of top teams with crisis challenges	• Well-balanced composition of perspectives (owners, executives, independent) • Continuous balancing of composition of professional profiles (functional and professional backgrounds, education, experience) • Access (and exit) mechanisms

Maintaining (or improving) the strategy process during crisis	• Create and maintain a specific strategy-making process
	  o Strategy decision-making committees
	  o Strategic audit
	• Incorporation of the external view (consultants, bankers, lawyers)
	• Continuous (but balanced) revision and formalization of decisions´ thresholds

Helping change the role of the CEO during crisis	• Check and balances of power (e.g. by increasing NED influence, empowering a lead director role or limiting CEO discretion) • CEO skill set in need of review
Develop internal board routines and procedures (also during crisis)	• Planning of boardroom activities across the year • Formal 'schedule' counterweights (agendas and TOCs, scheduling and calendars) • Evaluation of board performance
Other measures to increase board effectiveness during crisis	• Compensation alignment • The support of the institutional environment

Early assessment of crisis and timely reaction

A basic finding of our research about life at the apex talked about the fuzziness of the crisis concept in the boardroom. Crisis has an 'objective' and visible dimension at the macro (country or industry) level, for example: industry stagnation, increased unemployment, etc. At the same time, crisis has also an organizational dimension made of worsened business results, reduced slack in the reaction to the environment, increased competition against the focal firm and so on. However, crisis is also a socially enacted concept; it is perceived in different colors and intensities by different actors on the board and, hence, it is not univocal. Indeed, the recent economic and financial crisis has not been equally understood by all actors. It was often underestimated in intensity and duration, even at the individual boardroom unit of analysis.

Unity of action in the face of crisis might certainly help boards (and, therefore, their focal organizations) to tackle and fight crisis more effectively. In the face of crisis it is difficult to decide as a group, as an event can have different meanings for everyone and, in extreme cases, may not be not perceived by some of the actors in charge of taking decision and action. This equivocality has made it difficult for boards to react in a more structured and unified manner.[1]

Unity of action does not mean unity of views. Indeed, diversity of profiles and opinions may be difficult to handle, but if well managed

---

[1] A powerful metaphor, we think, is the idea of the canary in the coal mine. Caged birds (canaries) were used in the past by mining workers to show an early sign of the presence of dangerous gases such as carbon monoxide or methane (gas would first kill the bird, allowing a short lead-time for the mine workers to escape). Some type of early and non-debatable test to discern the intensity of crisis might have been extremely useful in the beginning of current financial crisis, for example, and might have reduced impact thereafter.

it helps to produce a richer view of the environment and, in the problem-solving process, by tackling 'groupthink' and generating new ideas (EC, 2011). A key discipline for organizations to tackle unexpected crisis effectively is being prepared for such events, but this crisis does seem to have taken many boards unprepared. Indeed, there might have been some kind of collective 'irrational exuberance' in the behavior of many economics actors.[2] Some of our sources even suggested that these bullish expectations might have been partially causal in the onset of crisis.

At the same time, several of our interviewees recognize that many directors misinterpreted the real intensity and duration of the current crisis. In addition to underestimating its importance, in most cases there were no formal crisis preparation protocols in place to react in the face of threatening events or, if there were, they were not as effective as they should have been.[3] Indeed, risk management done poorly can be as bad as no risk management at all (Frigo, 2009).

It is notable that most organizations represented in our research sample had not developed specific protocols or 'crisis toolkits' (and most probably have not yet, because fighting the crisis consumed—and still does—most available time and energy) to early warn future crisis events. This might mean that we have already planted the first seed for the next crisis or, at least, that

---

[2] Irrational exuberance is the famous expression Alan Greenspan (the then Federal Reserve head) used in December 1996 (during the dot-com bubble) to advise that the market might be overvalued.

[3] A proxy showing that these protocols were ineffective, in case they were actually in place, is the contradictory views many directors mention about the actual depth of crisis (or about its existence in the first place during the early stages). While diversity in the opinions to approach problem-solving may help enrich the solution, a late (or wrong) analysis increased crisis impacts for many organizations.

all needed surveillance systems to detect future downturn events are not yet in place. In fact, stronger organizational routines or crisis reaction protocols—such as a robust and well-known procedure of early detection (of crisis) and the initial action process in the face of crisis, both often related to strategy and risk assessment tools—might help to achieve an orchestrated reaction in front of this type of situation (Weick, 1993; Mitroff, Shrivastasa and Udwadia, 1987; Frigo, 2009).

These frameworks (crisis protocols) have the power to 'trigger' reaction in a more articulated manner, rather than leaving the reaction up for grabs of individual actors in the boardroom (particularly when the situation, as described previously, becomes particularly tense, and clear and collective thinking becomes more difficult). There could have been (and could be in the future) useful frameworks to react effectively in the face of crisis.

Besides the development of a crisis management model (Mitroff, Shrivastasa and Udwadia, 1987) or the development of a strategic risk management model (Frigo, 2009), there are a number of other factors that might potentially help boards more effectively handle crisis and minimize corporate effects. These are covered in the next sections.

Balancing composition of the top teams with crisis challenges

Larger boards are assumed to be more effective by the existing literature (Judge and Zeithaml, 1992). Research on team size suggests that teams are most effective when they have sufficient (but not greater than that) number of members to perform the group task (West and Anderson, 1996; Guzzo, 1988; Guzzo and Shea, 1992; Hackman, 1990). Decision quality is, in principle, contingent on the quality of the team taking the decision. The capacity of a team is thus, all things equal, related to the right size and composition of the team and, theoretically, this balanced composition in the boardroom is the first factor pushing towards wisdom and performance of top teams. It might be true that 'nobody is perfect; but a team can be', as suggested by Meredith Belbin (born 1926), British researcher and management theorist and the founder of the Belbin Team Role Inventory.

The traditional view on 'upper echelons' (Hambrick and Mason, 1984; Hambrick, 2007a) assumes that any organization is the 'reflection' of their leaders. From that perspective, a well-balanced composition of the directorate might indeed help to unify views at the organizational level and at board level (for example, through enough variety of backgrounds to achieve this balance). This heterogeneous (but poised to react) composition of the board might provide it with a rich enough view of the environment. Balance is not only achieved by mixing the right profiles (such as functional or educational background) but also mixing directors with different organizational interests and business perspectives—relative weight of independent and executive directors, for instance—so as to reach a well-rounded balance and perspective of all issues related to boardroom decision-making.

Establishing and maintaining a threshold of diversity in those dimensions or, at least, a targeted mix of the profiles of the board members, and then trying to enroll this mix, is definitely a crucial governance decision for the board to be effective, because it helps enrich boardroom activity and, in principle, promotes better quality of decisions (EC, 2011).

It is likely that rethinking board composition may also improve their ability to increase risk assumption levels, as a higher level of flexibility in top management and increased organizational resilience is said to be needed to face this new normality (McKinsey, 2008; 2009a; 2009b). For example, the enhancement and increasing importance of the lead director role (PWC, 2013), already present in a significant proportion of companies (PWC, 2011) and in many other areas of the world (PWC, 2010), may be an option to maintain board dynamics healthily 'isolated' from internal pressures in the company. To have an influential but theoretically independent role 'steering' the board besides the traditional (insider) formal roles—CEO, chairperson or board secretary—should strengthen board effectiveness and independence.

The richness and balance of skills in the boardroom is something that could be also used to evaluate managerial capacity on the side of the chairperson or CEO (as in their ability to lead a diverse group with different backgrounds and interests) and ultimately to assess overall board performance. From the perspective of diversity management, the role of the chairperson (and that of the lead director in some environments) becomes crucial to create useful dynamics in the boardroom and to leverage everyone's perspectives, including effective management of the balance of power.

In addition, access mechanisms are usually strong formally to protect independence (for example, proposed by a committee with, in principle, no chairperson/CEO influence) but they need to be continuously reassessed in order to reach this more balanced composition and to reduce indirect, but effective, influence of the CEO/chairperson in this type of recruiting decisions. This is so, because despite that the direct influence of the CEO/chairperson is notably 'diminished' by strong board institutions, such as the nomination and compensation committees, it still holds true that the first executive has many available resources to influence appointments and debate in the boardroom (McDonald and Westphal, 2013; Westphal and Khanna, 2003; Zajac and Westphal, 1996).

Warranting access to the boardroom only to the best suited for the role, regardless of any relationship with the focal chairperson or CEO, may indeed increase the actual independence of the boardroom. A different question is if this independence (Martin, 2011) is actually paying in terms of business performance, a critical but extremely difficult issue to be tested, as really independent directors may be in a worse position—due to asymmetry of management information and internal insight—to provide significant value to company governance. Despite these drawbacks, the use of an independent director (lead director) for critical board activities may provide the needed legitimacy to drill down in issues of directors' effectiveness and board performance and thus be effective to address the often complex issue of board continuous evaluation (PWC, 2013).

Nevertheless, the best team would not succeed without the right pattern of work, the right set of decision-making routines and the right decision-making process. This is covered in the following sections.

Maintaining (or improving) the strategy process under crisis

As noted in Chapter 3, short-termism is a clear trait of strategic decision-making during crisis. Crisis is about uncertainty and, inevitably, makes the strategy process more ambiguous. Indeed, its unanticipated nature is in the essence of crisis (Hermann, 1963). At the same time, embedded in the nature of crisis is a narrower scope of options or scenarios, because crisis is almost by definition related to more difficult problem-solving, reduced slack and increased scarcity of choice.

In addition, the pressure coming from crisis pushes the board towards more tactical considerations, and the risk of reducing the time and effort devoted to strategy is larger. Thus, 'forcing' the strategic agenda in the boardroom during crisis seems like a reasonable prescriptive move to prevent the board acting only in the supervision or sanction of tactical decisions and to maintain focus in strategic tasks. Strategy-making is, we think, at the core of the agenda that should remain 'stable' in boardroom activity across the years, even during crisis. Indeed, the paradox is, in the words of one of our sources, that 'the strategy process often tends to lose weight *precisely* when it is most needed (when opportunities are less, resources are scarcer and, thus, strategy decisions are more complex)' (emphasis added).

The importance of board attention to more tactical events during crisis seems prominent, showing a key difference with times of significant slack. Thus, one formal counterweight potentially useful to avoid excessive short-termism in this decision process is the creation (or enhancement) of devoted strategy-making processes and specific strategy committees to properly keep up and running this priority and to improve the quality of strategic decision-making, regardless of the uncertainty and ambiguity coming from the external environment. Importantly, we are not meaning necessarily here that this strategy committee (focus on strategy) should be formed by the same executive committee members (focus on day-to-day management execution) but that both should be operational and effectively coordinated.

To orient the board and maintain focus around the strategy process, Donaldson (1995) proposed the introduction of the 'strategic audit'. This is a useful tool to keep the board still attentive to longer-term plans and decisions and to reduce crisis-induced short-termism. Assessment tools such as evaluations of board performance (both as a group and individually) and strategic audits are, in principle, useful mechanisms to keep an eye on the longer run while solving operational issues, a balance that seems particularly crucial in the face of crisis.

The incorporation of external help (whether in the traditional form of external advisors—management consultants, bankers, lawyers, etc.—or semi-internal advisors, such as advisory boards or other type of advising committees) is a common method that large organizations use to enrich their decision-making process, attract external views and, eventually, balance short-term focus with longer-time plans. The timely involvement of these resources is a crucial issue in the face of crisis, even if all these groups are external constituencies and, thus, influencers but not themselves final decision makers.

Many large organizations formalize—via description of delegated discretion in their internal board statutes—which decisions should be taken within the board and, thus, which should not to be taken there, that is, those that could be taken by senior management below them. While this is a useful model, in theory, to balance workload for the board of directors, this dichotomy might be too rigid a division of tasks when there are high levels of external ambiguity; and to perform effectively during crisis there is a need of agile and continuous collaboration and overlapping of activities between the board and the executive team. This flexibility seems even more important during crisis than during expansion.

Helping to change the role of the CEO during crisis

Checks and balances in the boardroom are usually very important for the quality of the decision-making process. This is particularly remarkable during crisis and, from that perspective, the stance the CEO takes in the process is decisive due to his or her influence in the board team dynamics and composition.

A notable issue resulting from our research is the centralization propensity that boards experience during crisis. It has already been suggested that this centralization bias is largely caused by the risk aversion of decision makers and by the defense of their self-interests. This risk aversion is inherent to the increased ambiguity derived from crisis and may be often leveraged by the risk of external liabilities whether in the form of legal responsibilities—central during crisis because of increased perceived risk—or any other impending social punishment (such as impact on personal image or prestige). We need to admit that an excessive perception of risk may backfire (as in conflict of interest) by reducing actual independence and effectiveness (e.g. analysis paralysis).

Balancing centralization and control with empowerment is a difficult task. This balance is problematic particularly to serve the objective of help and surveillance of the management team (not their de facto 'replacement' via micromanagement). Crisis brings increased demands on the CEO and the board as a whole; providing the right balance between empowerment and control is a significant one. A good measure of leadership effectiveness in this situation seems to be the CEO ability to balance centralization and control with timely problem-solving.

Not surprisingly, CEO/chairperson character and required skills are even more crucial than in the previous expansion period. Table 7.2 shows a specific zoom, according to our sources, on chairperson/CEO required competences under crisis. We have organized these different capabilities into four main domains previously considered key in crisis literature for team leaders: strategic thinking, resource mobilization, effective execution and personal selflessness (Useem, Cook and Sutton, 2005).

TABLE 7.2 Required skillset for the CEO or executive chairperson during crisis (based on informants' views)

Strategic thinking	*Strategic making*	'During expansion every week there is a row of consultants and investment bankers queuing for a slot in your schedule to bring you exciting new ideas. Not during crisis. No one brings ideas and you have to think out and decide; make yourself the right question and find the right answer.' (CEO in a global firm)
	Analytical skills	'One of the crucial individual CEO characteristics is the ability to maintain cold analysis in the face of crisis.' (Chairman)
Ability to mobilize	*Talent management*	'A good chairman needs to manage (acquire, mobilize) the best talent he can during crisis.' (Independent Director)
	Team motivation	'It is crucial to maintain commitment of the executive team in the worst moment (more work, more tension and less pay).' (Proprietary Director of several companies)
	Communication skills	'During crisis, you (as a top executive) need communication skills both to create the momentum in your people and to communicate outside, particularly when it comes to listed companies.' (Independent Director)
Ability to execute	*Political savvy*	'During crisis, the chairman/CEO is more of a politician than a manager; always handling political equilibrium among parties.' (Executive Chairman, large European firm)
	Listening	'A wise CEO/chairman has to listen in this situation; more than ever.' (Independent Director)
	Toughness	'The CEO had to leave; he was very competent but not the style for crisis management.' (Executive Chairman) 'You have to motivate and protect key executive(s). You have less tools than ever (i.e. no extra money for compensation), situation is tougher and she can go nowhere because the market is collapsed.' (Executive Director)
	Other (decisiveness, pragmatism, results orientation, etc.)	'During crisis there are several crucial attributes for a CEO: A CEO has to be decisive, visible, pragmatic, able to accept mistakes, fair, results oriented, calm and organized.' (Chairman)

(continued)

TABLE 7.2 Continued

Personal selflessness	Self-confidence	'When things go badly you begin to hesitate about everything even about the ground you step on. And begin to wonder if you might have made mistakes before and what other competitors or companies are doing on a given topic.' (CEO in a large firm)
	Balance	'A good chairman/CEO is good in crisis or in expansion; simply the things to do and the tools are different. I dislike the pathological manager who creates crisis and tension when there is no reason for that. But precisely during crisis you need to stay quiet, the captain needs to be calm.' (Chairman)
	Trustworthiness	'A key CEO capacity is to create a team; to generate mutual trust and be part of a group endeavor: building trust with your directors is crucial.' (Former CEO and Independent Director)
	Ethics	'Not everything is valid to achieve results. The boundary is sometimes a thin line.' (Independent Director)
	Independence	'It is too often the fact that it is biology who retires the CEO or executive chairman; you have to stop before that in the best interest of the (focal) firm.' (external expert)
		'Only a handful of chairmen in firms listed in this market are independent according to regulator criteria, around xx%.' (external expert)

Maybe this grounded view is too demanding for just one character or person at the same time. Note that, in a way, interviewees are also projecting into these attributes their own romantic views of leadership that we mentioned in Chapter 1. However, the table seems beneficial to convey the variety of dimensions in which the CEO/chairperson should excel at—or be particularly decisive in—during crisis. Some of the assessment processes and tools we mentioned before (for instance, to assess the Board) might be useful for directors (and particularly the

CEO) in order to evaluate and nurture their managerial abilities to handle crisis.

Develop board decision-making routines and procedures (even during crisis)

Our sources hold that reaching a healthy equilibrium between confronting interests in the boardroom—those from owners, executives and external independent/non-executive directors— as well as among their professional backgrounds is healthy for board activities. Besides reaching a well-balanced composition of the directorate, maintaining a stable planning of board activities across the fiscal year is also needed during crisis. This aspect might have been particularly affected by the current economic downturn: even if we consider that the frequency and number of board meetings seems to have, in general, remained unchanged, crisis has often altered regular priorities in the boardroom, forcing the directorate to focus on more tactical issues and postponing all those activities more 'strategic' in nature.

The use of formal organizational mechanisms to keep this balanced activity in the boardroom, both in the form of predefined content (such as pre-planned and structured agendas) or in the form of stable routines, meeting scheduling and calendars for meetings, may help address the need for a more unified view of the external environment or of crisis itself. Key actors in this activity are usually the secretary of the board or the lead director, as they are typically a formal counterweight to the executive directors (and particularly the CEO) in maintaining a balanced planning of board activities across the fiscal year.

To be effective in this goal, entrenchment of a part of the board should be avoided and should not affect independence of judgment of directors as a whole. The aim should be to preserve the interest and stewardship of the focal company, rather than pushing only the views of a part or faction of the board. For example, the scheduling of board meetings and their contents should be planned sufficiently in advance, aligned with a coherent logic of the business cycles across the year, but inclusive of specific needs to be incorporated in these meetings, for instance reviews of exceptional results or other unplanned events across the fiscal year. This does not necessarily mean scheduling more board meetings, as this may be counterproductive for efficiency (García-Sanchez, 2010), but detaching the regular pace of life of boards from reactive or last minute priorities decided by the chairperson or CEO. Isolating the board from reactive priorities does not mean ignoring the regular business issues, but avoids having the board act as an amplifier of all 'business as usual' priorities, as this may make the board lose some emotional and technical 'distance' about decisions and avoid excessive (more than needed) centralization. At the same time, we also have to remember that it has been suggested before that too large a distance from directors to the 'real' company might have been partially causal of crisis, particularly when the issues under scrutiny were very technical or complex in nature (Davies, 2010).

Thus, it may be still needed to include regular board events or agenda content linked to the evolution of operations across the year, as well as to include 'unexpected' priorities into the board agenda, but preventing the board of directors to turn into 'firefighting' mode. In other words, the scheduling of board meetings should be connected with the evolution of the firm and the environment (for example, by monitoring business results) but should not work as a sounding board amplifying environmental threats or personal biases from executives. This means that, in many ways, the frequency and content of board activity could and should be defined upfront, but specifically adjusted to cover outstanding points or pressing business issues (as in those from crisis) within a pre-planned year or semester schedule of board activity. After all—and executive monitoring being one of the key roles that boards have to play—the 'regular' board dynamics should mirror executive action, including periodical activities such as budgeting, quarterly and annual closings and investment cycles. Many firms already use well-structured and thought-out board agendas and schedules, working with a pre-planned schedule flexible enough to gather incoming issues or urgent threats to performance. We believe that organizing and planning (flexibly) board activity pays via a more effective use of board resources (usually scarce), especially previous preparation and time spent by directors in board meetings. This includes planning and feeding properly the key historical information required by directors to perform their role, as well as *prospective information* (a significant demand by many of our interviewee board members). The diffusion of these planning practices across firms is expected as a consequence of crisis, because quality of board meetings is intimately related to the effectiveness of the board (Spencer Stuart, 2011) and organizations adopt new practices when they are considered proper to avoid legitimacy issues (DiMaggio and Powell, 1983).

Other measures to increase effectiveness of the board of directors during crisis

Having a board 'aligned' to the actual needs of the focal company is crucial: it is not always the case that a good director in expansion times is also the best choice for the downturn. Ultimately, the fit to the situation and management stature of directorates is more important than anything else; thus, the importance of other measures such as the evaluation of members of the board, both individually and collectively. The risk of implementation of these practices for those boards in which they are less frequent might be related to the tenure and maturity of directors, as well as to the internal power dynamics on the board, as evaluation might ultimately lead to changes in composition. Cultural differences among countries may also increase (or decrease) effort to implement these practices.

For the sake of stewardship, directors need to feel free to advise their focal boards. Given that independence appears as the 'key value' to protect, allowing the possibility for directors to be protected from their potential liabilities may be a valuable option to allow them to act freely. Our research suggests that there seems to be, for instance, an increased demand of civil insurance from directors during crisis in order to protect them from impending liabilities. Increasing directors' insurance, however, has to be analyzed in light of the potential counterproductive effects that this safeguard might have on them, such as promoting risk-seeking behaviors potentially destroying organizational value. This might affect decision-making and induce risk blindness to directors even if, at the same time, risk leverage could reduce effectiveness of directorates—via risk aversion—and even increase the scarcity of available talented independent directors due to excessive perceived personal exposure. There is, indeed, a recent but growing pressure for transparency and effectiveness of corporate governance, in part because senior management are seen as the culprits for many of the issues currently going on in the business community and affecting indirectly the rest of society. For instance, the exemplarity of managerial behavior has been in doubt after compensation issues in companies benefitted from state-funded bailouts, or because of some sense of distance from the rest of the workforce (CNNMoney, 2011; *The Guardian*, 2013b). The increasing social concern around these issues has reached the policy-making space and might bring also regulatory consequences. For example, some government and political parties in Europe demand new regulation to be applied to highly paid executives, such as asking for increases in the tax pressure for wealthy individuals (*The Economist*, 2011), or increasing measures to cap and limit executive compensation across Europe (*Financial Times*, 2013a; *Financial Times*, 2013b). A similar pressure is being observed in the US, although more timidly (*Washington Post*, 2011; *Financial Times*, 2013c). In addition, regulatory innovations passed as response to the late 2000s recession (such as the 2010 Dodd–Frank Wall Street Reform and Consumer Protection Act) pursue also stricter controls and increased liabilities for management in a monitoring intent with strong analogies to the former Sarbanes–Oxley Act (2002).

Without entering into the long debate on executive compensation, which is beyond the scope of this book, we notice how some compensation tools, such as claw-back clauses, are beginning to be used in many countries (University of Washington, 2011). These claw-back clauses protect, in principle, the organization from self-interested decisions of their board members or top executives by tying rewards to longer-term performance even retrospectively. The social pressure for the adoption of these new conditions (such as claw-back clauses in executive compensation) is growing. Indeed, by 2010, 82 percent of the Fortune 100 had voluntarily implemented claw-back clauses in their executive compensation contracts, up from just 18 percent in 2006 (University of Washington, 2011) and about one-third had thought to include this type of compensation clauses in executive pay schemes in the UK (*Financial Times*,

2011b). However, this practice may have significant drawbacks, such as the risk of non-legal security for those under that clause, and consequently it might be even considered illegal in some countries. At the same time, it may perversely influence executive behavior by, for instance, reducing risk assumption capacities.

Another substantial issue conditioning behaviors in the boardroom is the institutional environment. Regulators, the overall community of boards (such as institutional investors, proxy advisors, shareholders, etc.) and directors as well as the academia, ought to play a significant role in the improvement of existing standards of corporate governance. There are still significant differences in practice among developed countries in our environment (for a more detailed view, see Aguilera and Jackson, 2010).

These differences in practices across countries (Spencer Stuart, 2011) cover many dimensions (for instance board size, presence of women at the top, number of board meetings in the boardroom and compensation), but the most noticeable and most asymmetric are particularly those more strongly related with strengthened independence in the boardroom (thus, in principle, more relevant to recover from crisis). These are: (a) the dual role of chairperson, (b) the weight of independent directors in the boardroom and (c) the existence (or not) of a formal board evaluation process.

First, the dual role of the chairperson (as in concentrating CEO and chairperson positions) is more frequent (Spencer Stuart, 2011) in the USA (59 percent) and Spain (73 percent) by comparison to Italy (9 percent) or Great Britain (1.3 percent), with France in the middle (50 percent). Second, the weight of independent directors is highest in the USA (84 percent) while it is slightly higher than one-third (35 percent) in Spain, with Great Britain (57 percent) and France (54 percent) in the middle, and Italy (43 percent) closer to Spain (Spencer Stuart, 2011). Finally, a formal evaluation process in the boardroom seems positive to maintain competency and enhance independence in decision-making.

While this process (Spencer Stuart, 2011) is mostly universal in Anglo-Saxon (US and GB) firms and in France, the frequency in this process is smaller in Italy (73 percent) or Spain (81 percent) for large listed firms in Spanish IBEX and even smaller (60 percent) for other listed firms.

Regulators' influence may be essential. Regulations, codes and recommendations tend to be increasingly transversal or supranational, affecting a wider number of companies and countries and/or suggesting common conduct codes with increasing geographical influence (EC, 2011). Specifically, the monitoring and effective implementation of corporate governance codes (EC, 2011) may make the boards (and the companies they lead) more resilient to crisis. Effectiveness of corporate governance is, in fact, related to more successful boardroom decision-making under crisis. The role played by directors themselves, corporate consultants, business schools and academia to develop higher standards of quality in corporate governance could help boards face the current crisis and prepare organizations better for future crises.

What lies ahead

One of the challenges facing boards is whether or not we are learning enough out of the failures and difficulties of the current crisis or if, on the other hand, we may be generating the next wave of corporate failures via implementation delay to improvements of current corporate governance systems, or simply by not transforming enough existing corporate governance models.

Touching on this point, Martin (2011) suggests a complete revolution about corporate governance. He argues, quite persuasively, that current board functioning is a self-fulfilling prophecy: independent directors are burdened with the responsibility to defend the interest of stockholders, while they cannot compete in knowledge and capacity with internal executive directors. If they are independent, they must be outsiders and, as such, they are always in a worse position to add value to the focal firm. Boards' role, he continues, should be reinvented. From that perspective, boards should not be devoted to help companies obtain abnormally superior returns or to help companies in 'checking-the-box exercises', but rather should be devoted to just helping their companies perform well (Martin, 2011).

Some of the areas of possible prescription that we explored earlier in this chapter are already being put in practice by many companies, and plenty of them were already using these and other good practices even before the crisis. After all, healthy corporate governance is not more (but not less) than justly 'sharing' the agency costs of governing the organization and not allowing any single group or stakeholder in the organization to assume a significantly larger (or smaller) fraction of the cost than any other; it may be that the actual distribution of this agency cost has changed during these years of crisis, but not the need of making these agency costs acceptable for everyone.

On the other hand, we still need to better learn what brought us here. From that perspective, a deeper understanding about the origins and root causes of the current crisis, and new accounts about the nature of reactions in the boardroom, will help us better shape recommendations for corporate governance in the future and, in particular, to face future crises in the boardroom.

Conclusions

In this book we have made an attempt to interpret the differing boardroom voices that we collected from our interviewees on decision-making processes during crisis. It has been to a certain extent surprising to notice that romantic accounts of leadership in the boardroom during crisis have been almost completely replaced by narratives of frustration and skepticism. What emerges from the voices that we gathered is low independence of directors, the ongoing presence of flaws that contributed to the current crisis, and overall doubts on the quality of decision-making at the board level. This is, in itself, an effect of crisis changing the very perception of board members' daily job and experience. We make an effort to interpret these narratives by identifying and articulating what appear to be the key concepts in these narratives: perception of crisis, short-termism, centralization of decision-making, parochialism and self-interest. We wear the theoretical lenses provided by the garbage-can model of choice, which appeared to us the most suitable to understand decision-making process in the boardroom during crisis. Suitability of this model comes from our interviewees' accounts themselves, often narrating situations that were not in line with dominant economic rationality principles. Nevertheless, we cannot ignore that these concepts are seen by our sources as elements to react against, not as immutable conditions of board functioning. We believe this is a consequence of crisis too: the replacement of a certain board image (the one made famous by several movies and hero-like biographies for what boards actually do) seems to be on its way.

From a research perspective, despite limitations in the empirical data and sample, we believe that the arguments we derived are worth considering as a sound basis for further statistically significant examination, as they belong to a significant number of very high-profile insiders. Some data of these accounts indirectly suggest that firms under crisis often survive despite their boards, supporting the importance of highly skeptical theoretical stances about the actual effect of top management on firm performance.

Along with skepticism on the decision-making process, our sources warn that many factors producing the crisis (Davies, 2010) are still present within board decision-making processes. Following our interviewees, board effectiveness seems to be still part of the problem and not yet able to frame a way out of the current crisis. For this reason, our study ends up questioning some of the current arguments on decision-making processes. For instance, our study challenges the argument that centralization is driving effective monitoring or helping firms leave crisis faster. On the contrary, our research suggests that decision-making is postponed (and/or decision quality worsened) under over-centralized decision processes.

Both specialized and general communication media, and even the cinema, have lately echoed the inner life of top teams in large corporations under financial crisis. Crisis management from the boardroom perspective is also a timely topic for theorists and it is a burning matter in actual management practices. This topic has enormous relevance from the standpoints of the narrower board-related practitioners' and the wider society at large, due in part to the huge social implications of corporate leaders' decisions during crisis.

Our findings portray a very different boardroom picture compared to idealized descriptions of senior leadership. Risk aversion and self-interest seem to have more weight on decision-making processes than performance objectives. Symbolic representations of governance, rather than substantive decision-making manifestations, are frequent. During crisis, CEOs and directors seem to be concerned about their personal interests at least as much as they are about those of the firms they lead.

Everything seems to suggest that, as yet, the road for boards of directors to get out of crisis still needs a huge effort to be theorized and applied. If our sources are right, in the meantime, crisis could remain with the nuts and bolts of boardroom decision-making process, so continuing to produce negative effects on the economic system. If crisis is 'in the eye of the beholder', we have been told that boards still seem to look at crisis with the same old eyes.

Afterword

One of the most interesting issues for scholars, policymakers and practitioners, in what was initially a financial meltdown, then an economic crisis—and ultimately, in several countries, a political and institutional one—is the fact that these successive events took place well in the wake of the international wave of corporate governance reform implemented in the last decade of the past millennium and in the first years of the 2000s, including the Cadbury Report (1992), the Sarbanes–Oxley Act (2002), and many others (see Aguilera and Jackson, 2010 for a good account of the international diffusion of corporate governance reform). This globally varied set of reforms was intended to prevent precisely the type of crisis that spread throughout the West after the fall of Lehman Brothers in 2008. Those reforms were aimed at generating trust in the manner in which organizations were being run amongst shareholders and society at large, by way of enhanced responsibility and accountability and transparency—yet none of that was achieved. Moreover, and rather ironically, the financial crisis began precisely in the most regulated of all economic institutions: the banks, the industry most critical for the dissemination of trust throughout the economic system, its *pièce de résistance*.

Why did corporate governance reform fail? One explanation could be that the new regulations, mainly devised to monitor and oversee CEOs and boards, were insufficient or deficient. To a certain extent, law fails in effectively meeting reality. Alberto Lavín Fernández and Carmelo Mazza have contributed to this debate with an excellent work on the real dynamics of boards of directors and the deficient decision-making dynamics at work in them, which are characterized by centralism, parochialism and short-termism.

It is not the authors' hypothesis that the way boards function during crises diverges totally from the way they function in normal times, as if they were completely different modes. Their thesis, agreeing with that of the great maven of board dynamics, Harvard's Jay Lorsch (2012), is that crises exacerbate boards' poorest practices, with more dire consequences than during non-critical times. The best predictor of the quality of boards' decision-making during turbulent times is the quality of their processes during boom years. A crisis situation makes corporate governance much more challenging, but not qualitatively different from, governance in normal times.

Let me comment on the three main shortcomings that, according to Lavín Fernández and Mazza, boards exhibit in their decision-making dynamics when confronting a crisis.

'Short-termism' is not a phenomenon that takes place only at board level. Because boards are not isolated from what happens around them, they reflect, even spotlight, a trend towards short-term thinking intrinsic to the current economic and business system, a type of capitalism dominated by finance and the market logic of shareholders (Davis, 2009) who, especially with listed companies, are not generally committed to the company's long-term results. While they are legally proprietors, they do not display the more long-term concerns that one might expect from an owner, but rather the short-term focus of an investor. Short-termism is not, then, a problem unique to boards of directors, but, rather, a characteristic of today's capitalism, which cascades down to boards of directors due to the very rules that corporate governance reforms have promoted: shareholders should be represented on boards in such a way that they are not easily dominated by CEOs, and there should be 'independent' board members representing shareholders with marginal amounts of stock acquired in the stock market, who, due to collective action problems, cannot easily coordinate their preferences. That is, one could proffer the hypothesis that the corporate governance reforms that preceded the economic crisis of 2008 only served to aggravate short-termism.

Parochialism, the second of the common pitfalls boards fall into during times of prolonged distress, is an interesting phenomenon, the foundations of which are closely related to one of the anthropological assumptions of modern economics: self-interest, the main driver not only of the capitalist *homo oeconomicus*, but also of the democratic *homo politicus* As a consequence, the basic assumptions incorporated into failed corporate governance reforms are analogous to the fundamental conceptions about human beings embedded in democratic constitutions launched by the American Founding Fathers and the French Revolution. First, these conceptions posit that human beings tend to selfishly pursue their own individual good. Second, even if human beings wished to further the common good, this is cognitively impossible to comprehend and, in any case, if actually understood only dogmatism and authoritarianism would follow. Third, since human beings, once in power, tend to seek to accumulate more power, the best solution for designing political power structures is a division or balance of power, by which ambition counteracts ambition, one branch of power counteracts the other, that is, parochialism balances off other parochialisms. The logic is the same for corporate governance. For instance, the parochialism, as well as short-termism, of independent directors is offset by the supposedly longer-term perspective of executive directors; CEOs should not accumulate all the power and there should be a board chair. Thus, parochialism entails only the particular interests of different organizational actors, each of them with different stakes, intensified during a crisis situation. That is, there is no psychological solution, or hope for individuals with better motivations; but better regulations offer an (imperfect) alternative.

There are important arguments in this book that I would like to underscore, such as the vital distinction between short, intense crises—of the type upon which previous research has focused—and longer, more drawn-out and ambiguous crises, such as the one we are still witnessing in southern Europe, where the probabilities for an L-shaped exit to the crisis seem highly probable; or the very gradual, or incremental (in the best case) recovery of employment and high levels of growth as in the US. The authors have hit on the right target: corporate governance in a protracted crisis should be a key topic for research, and the study of economic and social policies to address such a situation the priority.

Science advances through systematic criticism within the academic community. It is, then, only fitting that I pose, in a spirit of collegiality, one comment for the authors to reflect upon as they proceed with their research. This involves their third bias: centralization. Reading the book one gets the impression that the authors conceive of centralization as an intrinsically negative trend. However, there is nothing necessarily positive or negative *per se* about centralization or, for that matter, decentralization. The effectiveness or fit of a particular structure and set of systems (such as information, control and decision-making) should be evaluated in accordance with the particular contingencies posed by the industry or the economic circumstances in question. Many companies in many industries during the years of economic prosperity maintained highly decentralized structures, and were able to sustain the increased costs that always accompany a decentralized organizational architecture. When competition intensified and the economic crisis set in and growth curves flattened, a good percentage of those highly decentralized companies adopted more centralized modes, most commonly through either light or full matrix structures, designs that could be sensible solutions under circumstances characterized by a lack of growth. Thus, centralization should not necessarily be viewed as a misguided decision by boards during crises. Rather, it merits criticism only when it is an inappropriate design for the specific structural contingencies of particular firms.

I will conclude this Afterword with two final comments. I'd like to praise the authors' excellent selection and splendid coverage of the organizational theory perspectives and schools that impinge on the topic. Also notable are their well-chosen quotations from the managers they interviewed as part of their research. It is a tribute to the researchers' interviewing ability how very telling these quotations are.

They also spark a thought-provoking theoretical question: most of the quotes in the book reveal that practitioners, at the senior management/ board levels, possess a strong understanding of the phenomena of short-termism, parochialism and centralization at the top in times of crisis. Of course, these practitioners do not employ an academic vocabulary—they do not need to—but they are insightful, incisive and articulately expressive. And yet while practitioners are knowledgeable about the phenomenon and the negative consequences it entails—and one could assume this is also the case with regulators and corporate governance experts—nothing seems to have been done, nor is being done, about it. That is, there is no systematic policy evaluation or proposals to improve the corporate governance reforms of the 1990s and early 2000s that failed so miserably to prevent the economic crisis that began in 2008. This probably means that the root of deficient board practices does not lie primarily at the individual level, with independent or dependent directors, CEOs, for example, but, rather, at group or organizational level, the ones the authors focus on, and even at the societal or institutional level. It is not, then, a question of motivation or competence or capabilities. It is a question of the quality of corporate governance regulation, about which the authors make a series of sensible recommendations in the final pages of the book.

José Luis Alvarez
Senior Associate Professor at INSEAD

References

Aguilera, R. V. and Jackson, Gregory (2003). 'The cross-national diversity of corporate governance: dimensions and determinants'. *Academy of Management Review*, 28(3), 447–465.

Aguilera, R. V. & Jackson, Gregory (2010). 'Comparative and international corporate governance'. *Academy of Management Annals*, 4(1), 485–556.

Allison, Graham & Zelikow, Phillip (1999). *Essence of Decision: Explaining the Cuban Missile Crisis*. 2nd edn. New York: Longman.

Alpasian, C., Green, S. & Mitroff, I. (2009). 'Corporate governance in the context of crises: towards a stakeholder theory of crisis management', *Journal of Contingencies and Crisis Management*, 17(1), 38–49.

Alvarez, J. L. & Svejenova, S. (2005). *Sharing Executive Power: Roles and Relationships at the Top*. Cambridge: Cambridge University Press.

Alvarez, J. L, Svejenova, S. & Vives, L. (2007). 'Leading in pairs'. *MIT Sloan Management Review*, 48(4), 10–14.

Amason, A. C. & Sapienza, H. J. (1997). 'The effects of top management team size and interaction norms on cognitive and affective conflict'. *Journal of Management*, 23, 495–516.

Amit, R. & Belcourt, M. (1999). 'HRM processes: a value-creating source of competitive advantage'. *European Management Journal*, 17(2), 174–181.

Ancona, D. & Caldwell, D. (1992). 'Demography and design: predictors of new product team performance'. *Organization Science*, 3(3), 321–341.

Atkinson, P. & Hammersley, M. (1994). 'Ethnography and participant observation'. In N. K. Denzin and Y. S. Lincoln (Eds.). *Handbook of Qualitative Research*. Thousand Oaks, CA: Sage Publications.

Axelrod, Robert (1984). *The Evolution of Cooperation*. New York: Basic Books.

Banco de España (2011). *Boletin Económico*. December 28.

Banerjee, A. V. (1992). 'A simple mode of herd behavior'. *Quarterly Journal of Economics*, 107(3), 797–817.

Bansal, Pratima & Corley, Kevin (2011). 'The coming of age for qualitative research: embracing the diversity of qualitative methods'. *Academy of Management Journal*, 54(2), 233–237.

Bantel, K. A. & Jackson, S. E. (1989). 'Top management and innovations in banking: does the composition of the top team make a difference?'. *Strategic Management Journal*, 10, 107–124.

Barnes, D. (1996). 'An analysis of the grounded theory method and the concept of culture'. *Qualitative Health Research*, 6(3), 429–441.

Baum, J. Robert & Wally, Stefan. (2003). 'Strategic decision speed and firm performance'. *Strategic Management Journal*, 24, 1107–1129.

BBVA Research, (2011). 'Algunas reflexiones sobre el escenario globaly previsional'.

BBVA Research, (2012). 'Global Outlook in the short and long run'. Group Chief Economist presentation to Deusto Business School Alumni, January.

BBVA Research. (2013). 'Situación EAGLES (Emerging and Growth Leader Economies'.

Becker, Markus C. (2004). 'Organizational routines: a review of the literature'. *Industrial and Corporate Change*, 13(4), 643–677.

Betsch, T., Brinkmann, J., Fiedler, K. & Breining, K. (1999). 'When prior knowledge overrules new evidence: adaptive use of decision strategies and the role of behavioral routines'. *Swiss Journal of Psychology*, 58, 151–160.

Betsch, T. S., Haberstroh, S., Glöckner A., Haar, T. & Fiedler, K. (2001). 'The effects of routine strength on adaptation and information search in recurrent decision making'. *Organizational Behavior and Human Decision Processes*, 84(1), 23–53.

Berg, S. V. & Smith S. K. (1978). 'CEO and board chairman: a quantitative study of dual vs. unitary board leadership'. *Directors and Boards*, 3, 34–39.

Blau, Peter. (1955). *The Dynamics of Bureaucracy: A Study of Interpersonal Relationships in Two Government Agencies*. Chicago: University of Chicago Press.

Bogert, J. D. (1996). 'Explaining variance in the performance of long-term corporate blockholders'. *Strategic Management Journal*, Research Notes and Communications, 17, 243–249.

Bourgeois, L. J. & Eisenhardt, K. M. (1988). 'Strategic decision processes in high velocity environments: four cases in the microcomputer industry'. *Management Science*, 34, 816–835.

Bromiley, Philip. (2005). *The Behavioral Foundations of Strategic Management*. Malden, MA: Blackwell Publishing.

Bushee, Brian. (1998). 'The influence of institutional investors on myopic R&D investment behavior'. *Accounting Review*, 73, 19–45.

Cameron, Kim S., Kim, Myung U. & Whetten, David A. (1987). 'Organizational effects of decline and turbulence'. *Administrative Science Quarterly*, 32, 222–240.

Cameron, Kim S., Whetten, David A. & Kim, Myung U. (1987). 'Organizational dysfunctions of decline'. *Academy of Management Journal*, 30, 126–138.

Cannella, Albert A. (2001). '*Upper echelons: Donald Hambrick on Executives and Strategy*'. *Academy of Management Executive*, 15(3), 36–42.

Cannella Jr., Albert A., Park, Jong-Hun & Lee, Ho-Uk. (2008). 'Top management team functional background diversity and firm performance: examining the roles of team member collocation and environmental uncertainty'. *Academy of Management Journal*, 51(4), 768–784.

Carmeli, Abraham. (2008). 'Top management team behavioral integration and the performance of service organizations'. *Group & Organization Management*, 33, 712–735.

Carpenter, Mason A., Fredrickson, James W. (2001). 'Top management teams, global strategic posture, and the moderating role of uncertainty'. *Academy of Management Journal*, 44(3), 533–545.

Carter, Nancy M. & Cullen, John B. (1984). 'A comparison of centraliza-tion/decentralization of decision making concepts and measures'. *Journal of Management*, 10(2), 259–268.

Chaganti, R. S., Mahajan, V., Sharma, S. (1985). 'Corporate board size, composition and corporate failures in the retailing industry'. *Journal of Management Studies*, 22, 400–417.

Chatterjee, A. and Hambrick, D. C. (2007). 'it's all about me: narcissis-tic CEOs and their effects on company strategy and performance'. *Administrative Science Quarterly*, September. 1346–1352.

Child, J. (1972). 'Organizational structure, environment and perfor-mance: the role of strategic choice'. *Sociology*, 6, 1–22.

Cho, Theresa S., Hambrick, Donald C. (2006). 'Attention as the mediator between top management team characteristics and strategic change: the case of airline deregulation'. *Organization Science*, 17(4), 453–469.

Choi, S. J., Fisch, J. E. & Kahan, M. (2008). 'Director elections and the influ-ence of proxy advisors'. NYU Center for Law, Economics and Organiza-tion. Law & Economics Research Paper Series, Working Paper, 08–22.

Cohen, Michael, March, James & Olsen, Johan. (1972). 'A garbage can model of organizational choice'. *Administrative Science Quarterly*, 17(1), 1–25.

Cohen, Michael & March, James. (1974; 1986). *Leadership and Ambigu-ity*. Boston: Harvard Business School Press.

Cohen, Michael, Burkhart, R., Dosi, G., Egidi, M, Marengo, L., Warglien, M. & Winter, S. (1996). 'Routines and other recurring action patterns of organizations: contemporary research issues'. *Industrial and Corporate Change*, 5, 653–698.

Conner, D. (1992). *Managing at the Speed of Change: How Resilient Managers Succeed and Prosper Where Others Fail*. New York: Villard Books/Random House.

Conyon, Martin J., Fernandes, N., Ferreira, M. A., Matos, P. and Murphy, K. J. (2012), 'The Executive Compensation Controversy: A Transatlantic Analysis'. In T. Boeri, C. Lucifora and K. Murphy (eds.), *Productivity, Profits and Pay*. Oxford: Oxford University Press.

Coombs, R. & Metcalfe, S. (2000). 'Universities, the Science Base and the Innovation Performance of the UK'. CRIC Briefing Paper No. 5. The University of Manchester & UMIST.

Corbin, J. & Strauss, A. (2008). *Basics of Qualitative Research*. Thousand Oaks, CA: Sage Publications.

CNN Money. (2011). 'Money for nothing at Goldman', http://finance.fortune.cnn.com/2011/01/30/money-for-nothing-at-goldman/.

Cross, Frank B., Tiller, Emerson H. (1998). 'Judicial partisanship and obedience to legal doctrine: whistleblowing on the federal courts of appeal'. *Yale Law Journal*, 107, 2155–2176.

Cyert, Richard M. & March, James G. (1963). *A Behavioral Theory of the Firm*. Upper Saddle River, NJ: Prentice-Hall.

Davidson, W., Nemec, C., Worrell, D. L. & Lin, Jun. (2002). 'Industrial origin of CEOs in outside succession: board preference and stockholder reaction'. *Journal of Management and Governance*, 6, 295–321.

Davies, H. (2010). *The Financial Crisis: Who Is To Blame?*. Cambridge: Polity Press.

Davis, Gerald F. (2009). *Managed by the Markets: How Finance Reshaped America*. Oxford: Oxford University Press.

DiMaggio, Paul J., Powell, Walter W. (1983). 'The iron cage revisited: institutional isomorphism and collective rationality in organizational fields', *American Sociological Review*, 48(2), 147–160.

Dobbin, Frank & Jung, Jiwook. (2010). 'The misapplication of Mr. Michael Jensen: how agency theory brought down the economy and why it might again'. Prepared for Markets on Trial: The Economic Sociology of the U.S. Financial Crisis. Edited by Michael Lounsbury & Paul M. Hirsch. Research in the Sociology of Organizations.

Donaldson, Gordon. (1995). 'New tool for boards: the strategic audit'. In *Harvard Business Review*, July/August. 99–107.

Driskell, James E. & Salas, Eduardo. (1991). 'Group decision making under stress'. *Journal of Applied Psychology*, 76(3), 473–478.

Drucker, Peter. (1954). *The Practice of Management*. New York: Harper & Row.

Dutton, J. E., Stumpf, S. A. & Wagner, D. (1990) 'Diagnosing strategic issues and managerial investment of resources.' *Advances in Strategic Management*, 6, 143–167.

Edmans, A. (2009). 'Blockholder trading, market efficiency and managerial myopia'. *Journal of Finance*, 64(6), 2481–2513.

Eisenhardt, Kathleen M. (1990) 'Speed and strategic choice: how managers accelerate decision making'. *California Management Review*. Spring. 39–54.

Eisenhardt, Kathleen M. (1992). 'High-reliability organizations meet high-velocity environments: common dilemmas in nuclear power plants, aircraft carriers and microcomputer firms'. In K. Roberts (Ed.). *New Challenges to Understand Organizations: High-Reliability Organizations*. Thousand Oaks, CA: Sage Publications.

Eisenhardt, K. M. & Bourgeois, L. J. III. (1988). 'Politics of strategic decision making in high velocity environments; towards a midrange theory'. *Academy of Management Journal*, 31, 737–770.

Eisenhardt, K. E. & Graebner, M. E. (2007). 'Theory building from cases: opportunities and challenges'. *Academy of Management Journal*, 50(1), 25–32.

Eisenhardt, K. M. & Zbaracki, M. J. (1992). 'Strategic decision making'. *Strategic Management Journal*, 13, 17–37.

Epstein, Lee, Landes, W. M. & Posner, R. A. (2011). 'Why (and when) judges dissent: a theoretical and empirical analysis'. *Journal of Legal Analysis*, 3/1, 101–137.

Erez, M. & Kanfer, F. (1983). 'The role of goal acceptance in goal-setting and task performance'. *Academy of Management Review*, 8, 454–463.

European Commission. (2011). 'Green paper: the EU corporate governance framework'. Brussels: COM, 164.

Enrione, A., Mazza, C. & Zerboni, F. (2006). 'Institutionalizing codes of governance beyond the boardroom's door: does change emerge from institutional pressures?'. *American Behavioral Scientist*, 49, 961–973.

Fetterman, D. M. (1998). *Ethnography: Step by Step*. Thousand Oaks, CA: Sage.

Feldman, M. S. (2003). 'A performative perspective on stability and change in organizational routines'. *Industrial and Corporate Change*, 12, 727–752.

Feldman, M. S. & Pentland B. T. (2003). 'Reconceptualizing organizational routines as a source of flexibility and change'. *Administrative Science Quarterly*, 48, 94–118.

Feldman, M. S. & Rafaeli, A. (2002). 'Organizational routines as sources of connections and understandings'. *Journal of Management Studies*, 39, 303–331.

Fich, E. M. & Shivdasani, A. (2006): 'Are busy boards effective monitors?' *Journal of Finance*, 61, 689–724.

Financial Reporting Council (FRC). (2010). *The UK Corporate Governance Code*.

Financial Times. (2011a). 'Repsol votes to ban Pemex from board'. 28 September.

Financial Times. (2011b). 'More companies to claw back executive pay'. 29 August.

Financial Times. (2012). 'Abramovich to take reduced Norilsk stake'. 12 December.

Financial Times. (2013a). 'Restraint in Europe', http://www.ft.com/intl/cms/s/0/dbd25610-aa52-11e2-bc0d-00144feabdc0.html.

Financial Times. (2013b). 'Boardroom pay model said to be "broken"'. http://www.ft.com/intl/cms/s/0/00289c56-9c69-11e2-ba3c-00144feabdc0.html.

Financial Times. (2013c). 'Companies: up in arms'. http://www.ft.com/intl/cms/s/0/4d3690b8-9d34-11e2-a8db-00144feabdc0.html.

Finkelstein, S. (1992). 'Power in top management teams: dimensions, measurement, and validation'. *Academy of Management Journal*, 35, 505–538.

Finkelstein, S. & D'Aveni, R. A. (1994). 'CEO duality as a double-edged sword: how boards of directors balance entrenchment avoidance and unity of command'. *Academy of Management Journal*, 37, 1079–1108.

Foldvary, Fred E. (2008). *The Depression of 2008*. Berkeley, CA: The Gutenberg Press.

Fontana, A. & Frey, James. (1994). 'Interviewing: the art of science'. In N. K. Denzin & Y. S. Lincoln (Eds.). *The Handbook of Qualitative Research*. Thousand Oaks, CA: Sage Publications.

Forbes. (2008). 'Fastest growing industries'. http://www.forbes.com/2008/09/26/fastest-growing-industries-lead-careers-cx_tw_0926jobgrowth.html.

Forbes, D. P. & Milliken, F. J. (1999). 'Cognition and corporate governance: understanding boards of directors as strategic decision-making groups'. *Academy of Management Review*, 24, 489–505.

Foss, Kirsten & Foss, Nicolai J. (2005). 'Resources and transaction costs: how property rights economics furthers the resource-based view'. *Strategic Management Journal*, 26(6), 541–553.

Freud, Sigmund. (1959). *Collected Papers*. New York: Basic Books.

Frigo, Mark L. (2009) 'Strategic risk assessment: the new core competency'. Balanced Scorecard Report, 11, No. 1, January–February.

Gaba, D. M., Maxwell, M. & DeAnda, A. (1987). 'Anesthetic mishaps: breaking the chain of accident evolution'. *Anesthesiology*, 66, 670–676.

Galbraith, John Kenneth (1954). *The Great Crash, 1929*. 3rd Edn. Boston: Houghton Mifflin.

García-Sánchez, I. M. (2010): 'The effectiveness of corporate governance: board structure and business technical efficiency in Spain'. *Central European Journal of Operations Research*, 18, 311–339.

Gavetti, G., Levinthal, D. & Ocasio, W. (2007). 'Neo-Carnegie: the Carnegie School's past, present, and reconstructing for the future'. *Organization Science*, 18(3), 523–536.

Geertz, C. (1973). *The Interpretation of Cultures*. New York: Basic Books.

Gephart, R. P. (2004). 'Qualitative research and the Academy of Management Journal'. *Academy of Management Journal*, 47, 454–462.

Gephart, R. P., Van Maanen, J. Jr. & Oberlechner, T. (2009). 'Organizations and risks in late modernity'. *Organization Studies*, 30, 141–155.

Gersick, Connie J. G. & Hackman, J. R. (1990). 'Habitual routines in task-performing groups'. *Organizational Behavior and Human Decision Processes*, 47, 65–97.

Gibbons, Robert. (2003). 'Team theory, garbage cans, and real organizations: some history and prospects of economic research on decision-making in organizations'. *Industrial and Corporate Change*, 12(4), 753–87.

Gladstein, Deborah L. & Reilly, Nora P. (1985). 'Group decision making under threat: the tycoon game'. *Academy of Management Journal*, 28(3), 613–627.

Glaser, Barney & Strauss, Anselm (1967). *The Discovery of Grounded Theory*. New York: Aldine de Gruyter.

Golden-Biddle, K. & Locke, K. (1993). 'Appealing work: an investigation of how ethnographic texts convince,' *Organization Science*, 4, 595–616.

Gore, Julie, Banks, Adrian, Millward, Lynne & Kyriakidou, Olivia (2006). 'Naturalistic decision making and organizations: reviewing pragmatic science'. *Organization Studies*, 27, 925–942.

Goulding, C. (1998). 'Grounded theory: the missing methodology on the interpretivist agenda'. *Qualitative Market Research: An International Journal*, 1(1) 50–57.

Graffin, S., Wade, J. Porac, J. & McNamee, R. (2008). 'The impact of CEO status diffusion on the economic outcomes of other senior managers'. *Organization Science*, 19, 457–474.

Granovetter, Mark (1985): 'Economic action and social structure: the problem of embeddedness. *American Journal of Sociology*, 3, 481–510.

Greenwood, R., Suddaby, Roy & Hinings, C. R. (2002). 'Theorizing change: the role of professional associations in the transformation of institutionalized fields'. *Academy of Management Journal*, 45(1), 58–80.

Guest, G., Bunce, A. & Johnson, L. (2006). 'How many interviews are enough?: an experiment with data saturation and variability'. *Field Methods*, 18, 59–82.

Gulati, R. & Singh, H. (1998). 'The architecture of cooperation: managing coordination costs and appropiation concerns in strategic aliances'. *Administrative Science Quarterly*, 43(4), 781–814.

Guzzo, R. A. (1988). 'Financial incentives and their varying effects on productivity'. In P. Whitney & R. B. Ochsman (Eds.). *Psychology and productivity*. New York: Plenum Press.

Guzzo, R. A. & Shea, G. P. (1992). 'Group performance and intergroup relations in organizations'. In M. D. Dunnette & L. M. Hough (Eds.). *Handbook of Industrial and Organizational Psychology*. Palo Alto, CA: Consulting Psychologists Press.

Hackman, J. R. (1990). *Groups That Work (and Those That Don't): Creating Conditions for Effective Teamwork*. San Francisco: Jossey-Bass.

Hage, Jerald & Aiken, Michael. (1966). 'Organizational alienation: a comparative analysis'. *American Sociological Review*, 31(4), 497–507.

Hage, Jerald & Aiken, Michael. (1967). 'Relationship of centralization to other structural properties'. *Administrative Science Quarterly*, 12, 72–93.

Haleblian, J, Devers, C. E., McNamara, G., Carpenter, M. A. & Davison, R. B. (2009). 'Taking stock of what we know about mergers and acquisitions: a review and research agenda'. *Journal of Management*, 35, 469–502.

Haleblian, J. & Finkelstein, Sydney (1993). 'Top management team size, CEO dominance and firm performance: the moderating roles of environmental turbulence and discretion'. *Academy of Management Journal*, 36(4), 844–863.

Hambrick, D. C. (1994). 'Top management groups: a conceptual integration and reconsideration of the 'team' label/research in organizational behavior'. In B. M Staw & L. L. Cummings (Eds.). 'Research in organization behavior', 16, 171–214.

Hambrick, D. C. (1995). 'Fragmentation and the other problems CEOs have with their top management teams'. *California Management Review*, 37(3), 110–127.

Hambrick, D. C. (1998). 'Corporate coherence and the top management team'. In D. C. Hambrick, D. A. Nadleer & M. L. Tushman (Eds.). *Navigating Change: How CEOs, Top Teams, and Boards Steer Transformation*. Boston, MA: Harvard Business School Press.

Hambrick, D. C. (2007a). 'Upper echelons theory: an update'. *Academy of Management Review*, 32(2), 334–343.

Hambrick, D. C. (2007b). 'The field of management´s devotion to theory: too much of a good thing?'. *Academy of Management Journal*, 50(6), 1346–1352.

Hambrick, D. C., Cho T. S. & Chen, M. (1996). 'The influence of top management team heterogeneity on firms' competitive moves'. *Administrative Science Quarterly*, 41, 659–684.

Hambrick, D. C., Geletkanycz, M. A. & Fredrickson, J. W. (1993). 'Top executive commitment to the status quo: some test of its determinants', *Strategic Management Journal*, 14, 401–418.

Hambrick, D. C. & Mason, P. (1984). 'Upper echelons: the organizations as a reflection of its top managers'. *Academy of Management Review*, 9, 193–206.

Hambrick, D. & Pettigrew, A. (2001). 'Upper echelons: Donald Hambrick on executives and strategy'. *Academy of Management Executive*, 15(3), 36–44.

Hannan, M. T. & Freeman, J. (1977). 'The population ecology of organizations'. *American Journal of Sociology*, 82(5), 929–964.

Hannan, M. T. & Freeman, J. (1984). 'Structural inertia and organizational change'. *American Sociological Review*, 49 (April), 149–164.

Harshbarger, D. (1971). 'An investigation of a structural model of small group problem solving'. *Human Relations*, 14, 43–63.

Hayward, M. L. A & Hambrick, D. (1997). 'Academic journal explaining the premiums paid for large acquisitions: evidence of CEO hubris'. *Administrative Science Quarterly*, 42(1), 103–127.

Hayward, M. L. A., Rindova, V. P. & Pollock, T. G. (2004). 'Believing one's own press: the causes and consequences of CEO celebrity'. *Strategic Management Journal*, 25(7), 637–653.

Hayward, M. L. A., Shepherd, D. A. & Griffin, D. W. (2006). 'A hubris theory of entrepreneurship'. *Management Science*, 52, 160–172.

Healy, P. & Wahlen, J. (1999). 'A review of the earnings management literature and its implications for standard setting'. *Accounting Horizons*, 13(4), 365–383.

Hermann, C. F. (1963). 'Some consequences of crisis which limit the viability of organizations'. *Administrative Science Quarterly*, 8: 61–82.

Hiller, N. & Hambrick, D. C. (2005). 'Conceptualizing executive hubris: the role of (hyper)- core self-evaluations in strategic decision-making'. *Strategic Management Journal*, 26, 297–319.

Hillman, A. J., Cannella, Jr, Albert A. & Paetzold, R. L. (2000) 'The resource dependence role of corporate directors: strategic adaptation of board composition in response to environmental change'. *Journal of Management Studies*, 37(2), 235–256.

Hillman, A. & Dalziel, T. (2003). 'Boards of directors and firm performance: integrating agency and resource dependence perspectives', *Academy of Management Review*, 28, 383–396.

HKP. (2012). 'Executive and non executive director compensation in Europe 2011/2012'. HKP, company website: http://www.hkp.com/en/publications/newsletter/newsletter961.html.

Holroyd, K. A. & Lazarus, R. S. (1982). 'Stress, coping, and somatic adaptation'. In L. Goldberger & S. Breznitz (Eds.). *Handbook of Stress: Theoretical and Clinical Aspects*. New York: Free Press.

Holt, Charles A. & Laury, Susan K. (2002). 'Risk aversion and incentive effects'. *American Economic Review*, 92(5), 1644–1655.

Jackall, Robert. (1988). *Moral Mazes: The World of Corporate Managers*. Oxford: Oxford University Press.

Janis, I. L. (1982). *Groupthink*. 2nd edn. Boston, MA: Houghton–Mifflin.

Jensen, M. C. (1986) 'Agency costs of free cash flow, corporate finance and takeovers', *American Economic Review*, 76(2), 323–329.

Jensen, M. & Zajac, E. J. (2004). 'Corporate elites and corporate strategy: how demographic preferences and structural position shape the scope of the firm'. *Strategic Management Journal*, 25(6), 507–524.

Johnson, J. L., Daily, C. M., & Ellstrand, A. E. (1996). 'Boards of directors: a review and research agenda'. *Journal of Management*, 22, 409–438.

Jones, Oswald & Craven, Martin. (2001): 'Beyond the routine: innovation management and the Teaching Company Scheme'. *Technovation*, 21, 267–279.

Judge, W. & Zeithaml, Carl P. (1992). 'Institutional and strategic choice perspectives on board involvement in the strategic decision process'. *Academy of Management Journal*, 35(4), 766–794.

Julian, S. D. & Ofori-Dankwa, J. (2008). 'Towards an integrative cartography of two strategic issue diagnosis frameworks'. *Strategic Management Journal*, 29, 93–114.

Kahneman, D., Slovic, P. & Tversky, A. (Eds.). (1982). *Judgment Under Uncertainty: Heuristics and Biases*. New York: Cambridge University Press.

Ketokivi, M. & Mantere, S. (2010). 'Two strategies for inductive reasoning in organizational research'. *Academy of Management Review*, 35(2), 315–333.

Kupperman, R., Wilcox, R. & Smith, H. A. (1975). 'Crisis management: some opportunities'. *Science*. 187(4175), 404–410.

La Porte, T. & Consolini, P. (1991). 'Working in practice but not in theory: theoretical challenges of "high-reliability organizations"'. *Journal of Public Administration Research and Theory: J-PART*, 1(1), 19–48.

Laverty, K. J. (1996). 'Economic "short-termism": the debate, the unresolved issues, and the implicationsfor management practice and research'. *Academy of Management Review*, 21 (3), 825–860.

Lawrence, P. & Lorsch, J. (1967). 'Differentiation and integration in complex organizations'. *Administrative Science Quarterly*, 12, 1–30.

Lawrence, T. & Suddaby, Roy. (2006). 'Institutions and institutional work'. In S. Clegg, C. Hardy, W. R. Nord & T. Lawrence (Eds.), *Handbook of Organization Studies*. London: Sage.

Lawrence, Tom, Suddaby, Roy & Leca, Bernard. (2009) 'Institutional work: an introduction. In Tom Lawrence, Roy Suddaby & Bernard Leca (Eds.), *Institutional Work*. Cambridge: Cambridge University Press.

Lazarus, Richard S. & Folkman, Susan. (1984). *Stress, Appraisal and Coping*. New York: Springer.

Leveson, Nancy, Dulac, Nicolas, Marais, Karen & Carroll, John. (2009). 'Moving beyond normal accidents and high reliability organizations: a systems approach to safety in complex systems'. *Organization Studies*, 30(2&3), 227–249.

Levinthal, Daniel A. (2012). 'From the ivy tower to the C-suite: garbage can processes and corporate strategic decision making'. In Alessandro Lomi & J. Richard Harrison (Eds.), *The Garbage Can Model of Organizational Choice: Looking Forward at Forty* (Research in the Sociology of Organizations, Volume 36). Emerald Group.

Levitt, B. & Nass, C. (1989). 'The lid on the garbage can: institutional constraints on decision making in the textbook publishing industry'. *Administrative Science Quarterly*, 34(2), 190–207.

Locke, K. (2001). *Grounded Theory in Management Research*. London: Sage.

Lomi, Alessandro & Harrison, J. Richard. (2012). 'The garbage can model of organizational choice: looking forward at forty'. In Alessandro Lomi & J. Richard Harrison (Eds.), *The Garbage Can Model of Organizational Choice: Looking Forward at Forty* (Research in the Sociology of Organizations, Volume 36). Bingley, UK: Emerald Group Publishing Limited.

Lorsch, Jay (Ed.) (2012). *The Future of Boards: Meeting the Governance Challenges of the XXI Century*. Boston, MA: Harvard Business School Press.

Lorsch, J. W. & MacIver, Elizabeth (1989). *Pawns or Potentates: The Reality of America's Corporate Boards*. Boston, MA: Harvard Business School Press.

Lounsbury, M. (2007). 'Tale of two cities: competing logics and practice variation in the professionalizing of mutual funds'. *Academy of Management Journal*, 50(2), 289–307.

McDonald, Michael & Westphal, James D. (2013). 'Access denied: low mentoring of women and minority first-time directors and its negative effects on appointments to additional boards'. *Academy of Management Journal*, 56(4), 1169–1198.

McDonald, M., Khanna, P. & Westphal, J. D. (2008). 'Getting them to think outside the circle: corporate governance, CEO advice networks, and firm performance'. *Academy of Management Journal*, 51, 453–475.

McKinsey. (2008). 'Leading through uncertainty'. *The McKinsey Quarterly*, December, 2008.

McKinsey. (2009a). 'The new normal'. *The McKinsey Quarterly*, March 2009.

McKinsey. (2009b). 'Dynamic management: better decisions in uncertain times'. *The McKinsey Quarterly*, December 2009.

March, J. G. (1988). *Decisions and Organizations*. Oxford: Basil Blackwell.

March, J. G. (1994). *A Primer On Decision Making: How Decisions Happen'*. New York: The Free Press.

March, J. G. & Simon, H. (1958). *Organizations*. Cambridge, MA: Blackwell Business.

March, J. G. & Olsen, J. P. (1976). *Ambiguity and Choice in Organizations*. Bergen: Universitetsforlaget.

March, J. G. & Olsen, J. P. (1995). *Democratic Governance*. New York: Free Press.

March, J. G. & Weissinger-Baylon, R. (1986). *Ambiguity and Command*. White Plains, NY: Longman.

Marginson, D. & McAulay, L. (2008). 'Exploring the debate on short-termism: a theoretical and empirical analysis'. *Strategic Management Journal*, 29(3), 273–292.

Marsh, Robert M. (1992). 'A research note: centralization of decision-making in Japanese factories'. *Organization Studies*, 13(2), 261–274.

Martin, R. L. (2011). *Fixing the Game*. Harvard Business School Press.

Mayer, R. C. & Gavin, M. B. (2005). 'Trust in management and performance: who minds the shop while the employees watch the boss?'. *Academy of Management Journal*, 48, 874–888.

Mechanic, David. (1962). 'Organizational power of lower participants'. *Administrative Science Quarterly*, 7, 349–365.

Meindl, J. R., Ehrlich, S. B. & Dukerich, J. M. (1985). 'The romance of leadership'. *Administrative Science Quarterly*, 30, 78–102.

Meyer, John W. & Rowan, Brian. (1977) 'Institutionalized organizations: formal structure as myth and ceremony'. *American Journal of Sociology*, 83(2), 340–363.

Meyer, J. W. & Rowan, B. (1983). 'The structure of educational organizations'. In J. W. Meyer & W. R. Scott (Eds.). *Organizational Environments: Ritual and Rationality*. Beverly Hills, CA: Sage.

Milburn, T. W., Schuler, R. & Watman, K. H. (1983). 'Organizational crisis: definition and conceptualization'. *Human Relations*, 36, 1141–1180.

Miles, M. B. & Huberman, A. M. (1994). *Qualitative Data Analysis*. 2nd edn. Thousand Oaks, CA: Sage.

Minto, Barbara (1996). *The Minto Pyramid Principle: Logic in Writing, Thinking, and Problem Solving'*. London: Pitman Publishing, Financial Times.

Mintzberg, H. (1973). *The Nature of Managerial Work'*. New York: Harper & Row.

Mishra, Aneil K. (1996). 'Organizational responses to crisis: the centrality of trust'. In Roderick M. Kramer and Thomas Tyler (Eds.). *Trust in Organizations*. Newbury Park, CA: Sage.

Mitroff, I. I., Shrivastasa, P. & Udwadia, F. E. (1987). 'Effective crisis management'. *The Academy of Management Executive*, 1(4), 283–292.

Mizruchi, Mark S. (1996). 'What do interlocks do? an analysis, critique, and assessment of research on interlocking directorates'. *Annual Review of Sociology*, 22, 271–298.

Mosakowski, E. (1997). 'Strategy making under causal ambiguity: conceptual issues and empirical evidence'. *Organization Science*, 8(4), 414–442.

Nelson, R. R. & Winter, S. G. (1982). *An Evolutionary Theory of Economic Change*. Cambridge, Mass. Belknap Press of Harvard University Press.

Niiniluoto, I. (1999) 'Defending abduction'. *Philosophy of Science*. 66(3), S436–S451.

New York Times. (2011). 'Confident deal makers pulled out checkbooks in 2010'. 3 January.

Ocasio, William (1995). 'The enactment of economic adversity: a reconciliation of theories of failure-induced change and threat rigidity'. *Research in Organizational Behavior*, 17, 287–331.

Ocasio, William (1999). 'Institutionalized action and corporate govern-ance: the reliance on rules of CEO succession'. *Administrative Science Quarterly*, 44, 384–416.

OECD. (2010). 'Corporate Governance and the Financial Crisis'.

Oliver, C. (1992). 'The antecedents of deinstitutionalization', *Organiza-tion Studies*, 13, 563–588.

O'Reilly, C. A., Snyder, R. C., & Boothe, J. N. (1993). 'Executive team demo-graphy and organizational change'. In Hunter, G. P. & Glick, W. H. (Eds.), *Organizational Change and Redesign: Ideas and Insights for Improving Performance*. New York: Oxford University Press.

Padgett, J. F. (1980). 'Managing garbage can hierarchies'. *Administra-tive Science Quarterly*, 25(4), 583–604.

Paroutis, Sotirios & Pettigrew, Andrew. (2007). 'Strategizing in the multibusiness firm: strategy teams at multiple levels and over time'. *Human Relations*, 60(1), 99–135.

Pearson, C. M. & Clair, J. A. (1998). 'Reframing crisis management'. *Academy of Management Review*, 23(1), 59–76.

Pearson, C. & Mitroff, I. (1993). 'From crisis prone to crisis prepared: a framework for crisis management'. *Academy of Management Executive*, 7(1), 48–59.

Peirce, C. S. (1931). *Collected Papers of Charles Sanders Peirce*, ed. Charles Hartshorne and Paul Weiss. Oxford University Press.

Pentland, B. T. (1995) 'Grammatical models of organizational proces-ses.' *Organization Science*, 6, 541–556.

Pentland, B. T. & Rueter, H. H. (1994). 'Organizational routines as grammars of action'. *Administrative Science Quarterly*, 39, 484–510.

Perrow, C. (1986) [1972]. *Complex Organizations: A Critical Essay.* New York: Random House.

Perrow, C. (1994). 'The limits of safety: the enhancement of a theory of accidents'. *Journal of Contingencies and Crisis Management,* 2(4), 212–220.

Pettigrew, A. M. (1992): 'On studying corporate elites'. *Strategic Management Journal,* 13, 337–348.

Pfeffer, Jeffrey (1978). *Organizational Design.* Arlington Heights, IL: Harlan Davidson.

Pfeffer, Jeffrey (1981). *Power in Organizations.* Marshfield, MA: Pitman.

Pfeffer, Jeffrey (1983). 'Organizational demography'. In L. L. Cummings and Barry M. Staw (Eds.). *Research in Organizational Behavior,* 5. Greenwich, CT: JAI Press.

Pfeffer, J. & Salancik, G. R. (1978). *The External Control of Organizations: A Resource Dependence Perspective.* New York: Harper and Row.

Pi, L., & Timme, S. G. (1993). 'Corporate control and bank efficiency'. *Journal of Banking and Finance,* 17, 515–530.

Pissarides, C. (2011). 'The future of employment in Europe'. Public Speech, October, Fundación Rafael del Pino.

Polanyi, Karl. (1957). *The Great Transformation.* Boston: Beacon Press.

Poulton, B. C. (1995). 'Effective multidisciplinary teamwork in primary health care'. Institute of Work Psychology, University of Sheffield, Sheffield, England.

Powell, T. C., Lovallo, D. & Caringal, C. (2006). 'Causal ambiguity, management perception, and firm performance'. *Academy of Management Review,* 31, 175–196.

Powell, Walter W. & DiMaggio, Paul J. (1991). 'Introduction'. In Walter W. Powell and Paul J. DiMaggio (Eds.) *The New Institutionalism in Organizational Analysis.* Chicago: University of Chicago Press.

Power, Michael (1996). *The Audit Society: Rituals of Verification.* Oxford University Press.

Pugh, D. S., Hickson, D. J., Hinings, C. R., MacDonald, K. M., Turner, C. & Lupton, T. (1963). 'A conceptual scheme for organizational analysis'. *Administrative Science Quarterly,* 8, 289–315.

Purdy, J. M. & Gray, B. (2009). 'Conflicting logics, mechanisms of diffusion and multilevel dynamics in emerging institutional fields'. *Academy of Management Journal*, 52(2), 355–380.

PWC (2010). 'Lead directors: A study of their growing influence and importance'. April.

PWC (2011). 'Consejos de Administración de Empresas Cotizadas, España'. Junio.

PWC (2013). 'PWC's annual corporate directors survey. Boards confront an evolving landscape'.

Pye, Annie & Pettigrew, Andrew (2005). 'Studying board context, process and dynamics: some challenges for the future'. *British Journal of Management*, 16, S27–S38.

Quack, S., Morgan, G. & Whitley, R. (2000). *National Capitalisms, Global Competition and Economic Performance*. Amsterdam and Philadelphia: Benjamins.

Quinn, Kevin M. (2012). 'The academic study of decision making on multimember courts'. *California Law Review*, 1445.

Ranson, S., Hinings, B. & Greenwood, R. (1980). 'The structuring of organizational structures'. *Administrative Science Quarterly*, 25 (1), 1–17.

Rechner, P. L. & Dalton, D. R. (1989). 'The impact of CEO as board chairperson on corporate performance: evidence vs. rhetoric'. *Academy of Management Executive*, 3(2), 141–143.

Rechner, P. L. & Dalton, D. R. (1991). 'CEO duality and organizational performance: a longitudinal analysis'. *Strategic Management Journal*, 12(2): 155–160.

Revesz, Richard L. (1997). 'Environmental Regulation, Ideology, and the D.C. Circuit'. *Virginia Law Review*, 83(8), 1717–1772.

Roberts, K. H. & Bea, R. (2001). 'Must accidents happen? Lessons from high-reliability organisations'. *Academy of Management Executive*, 15(3), 70–79.

Roberts, K. H., Stout, S. K. & Halpern, J. J. (1994) 'Decision dynamics in two high reliability military organizations'. *Management Science*, 40(5), 614–624.

Romney, A. K., Weller, S. C. & Batchelder, W. H. (1986). 'Culture as consensus: a theory of culture and informant accuracy'. *American Anthropologist*, 88, 313–338.

Rose, Andrew K. & Spiegel, Mark M. (2010). 'Cross-country causes and consequences of the 2008 crisis: international linkages and American exposure'. *Pacific Economic Review*, 15(3), 340–363.

Rose, Andrew K. & Spiegel, Mark M. (2011). 'Cross-country causes and consequences of the crisis: an update'. Working Paper Series 2011–02, Federal Reserve Bank of San Francisco.

Rumelt, Richard P. (1995). 'Inertia and Transformation'. In Cynthia A. Montgomery (Ed.) *Resources in an Evolutionary Perspective: Towards a Synthesis of Evolutionary and Resource-Based Approaches to Strategy*. Norwell, MA: Kluwer Academic.

Samuel, Cherian (2000). 'Does shareholder myopia lead to managerial myopia? A first look'. *Applied Financial Economics*, 10(5), 493–505.

Samuel, Cherian (2001). 'Stock market and investment: the signaling role of the market'. *Applied Economics*, 33(10), 1243–1252.

Sánchez-Marín, G., Baixauli-Soler, J. S. & Lucas Pérez, M. E. (2010). 'When much is not better? Top management compensation, board structure, and performance in Spanish firms'. *International Journal of Human Resource Management*, 21, 2776–2795.

Schraagen, J. M, Huis in 't Veld, M. & de Koning, L. (2010). 'Information sharing during crisis management in hierarchical vs. network teams'. *Journal of Contingencies and Crisis Management*, 18(2), 117–127.

Sharma, Monika & Ghosh, Anjali (2007). 'Does team size matter? A study of the impact of team size on the transactive memory system and performance of IT sector teams'. *South Asian Journal of Management*, 14(4), 96–115.

Sharot, T., Delgado, M. R. & Phelps, E. A. (2004). 'How emotion enhances the feeling of remembering'. *Nature Neuroscience*, 7(12), 1376–1380.

Sheridan, T. B. (1981). 'Understanding human error and aiding human diagnostic behavior in nuclear power plants'. In J. Rasmussen & W. B. Rouse (Eds.). *Human Detection and Diagnosis of System Failures*. New York: Plenum.

Simon, Herbert A. (1997) [1945, 1947, 1957, 1961, 1976]. *Administrative Behavior: A Study of Decision-Making Processes in Administrative Organizations*. 4th edn. New York; The Free Press/Simon & Schuster.

Simons, T., Pelled, L. H. & Smith, K. A. (1999). 'Making use of difference: diversity, debate, and decision comprehensiveness in top management teams'. *Academy of Management Journal*, 42, 662– 675.

Simsek, Zeki, Veiga, John F., Lubatkin, Michael H. & Dino, Richard N. (2005). 'Modeling the multilevel determinants of top management team behavioral integration'. *Academy of Management Journal*, 48(1), 69–84.

Smart, C. & Vertinsky, I. (1977). 'Design for crisis decision units'. *Administrative Science Quarterly*, 22, 640–657.

Smart, C. & Vertinsky, I. (1984). 'Strategy and the environment: a study of corporate responses to crisis'. *Strategic Management Journal*, 5, 199–213.

Smith, K. G., Smith, K. A., Olian, J. D., Sims, H. P., O´Bannon, D. P. & Scully, J. A. (1994). 'Top management team demography and process: the role of social integration and communication'. *Administrative Science Quarterly*, 39, 412–438.

Snook, Scott A. (2000). *Friendly Fire: The Accidental Shootdown of U.S. Black Hawks Over Northern Iraq*. Princeton, NJ: Princeton University Press.

Spencer, Stuart. (2011). *España 2011: Indice Spencer Stuart de Consejos de Administración*, 15ª Edición. Madrid: Spencer Stuart.

Spitzer, Matthew & Talley, Eric. (2011). 'Left, right and center: strategic information acquisition and diversity in judicial panels', J. L. Economy and Organization, http://jleo.oxfordjoumals.org/content/early/2011/09/14/jleo.ewiO13.fuli:pdf,doi:10.1093/jleo/ewiO13.

Sridharan, U. V. & Marsinko, A. (1997). 'CEO duality in the paper and forest products industry'. *Journal of Financial and Strategic Decisions*, 10(1), 59–65.

Starbuck, W. & Hedberg, B. L. T. (1977). 'Saving an organization from stagnating environment'. In H. Thorelli (Ed.) *Strategy + structure = performance: 249–258*, Bloomington, IN: Indiana University Press.

Staw, B. M., Sandelands, L. E. & Dutton, J. E. (1981). 'Threat-rigidity effects in organizational behavior: a multi-level analysis'. *Administrative Science Quarterly*, 26, 501–524.

Strauss, Anselm & Corbin, Juliet (1998). *Basics of Qualitative Research Techniques and Procedures for Developing Grounded Theory.* 2nd edn. London: Sage.

Suddaby, R. (2006). From the editors: 'What grounded theory is not'. *Academy of Management Journal,* 49, 633–642.

Taylor, John (2009). *Wall Street Journal,* 9 February,. http://online.wsj. com/article/SB123414310280561945.html.

Teece, D. J. & Pisano, G. (1994). 'The dynamic capabilities of firms: an introduction'. *Industrial and Corporate Change,* 3(3), 537–556.

The Atlantic. (2011). '12 Industries that are actually growing'. http:// www.theatlantic.com/business/archive/2011/02/12-industries-that-are-actually-growing/70641/#slide1.

The Economist. (2011). 'Hunting the rich', http://www.economist. com/node/21530104

The Guardian. (2013a). http://www.theguardian.com/business/2013/ mar/04/non-executive-ftse-pay-rises.

The Guardian. (2013b). http://www.theguardian.com/business/2013/ jul/01/bosses-award-bonuses-workers-pay-rise.

The Independent. (2013). 'Mark Leftly: how guerrilla tactics are forcing boardrooms to man the battle stations'. http://www.independent. co.uk/news/business/comment/mark-leftly-how-guerrilla-tactics-are-forcing-boardrooms-to-man-the-battle-stations-8612115.html.

Thornton, P. H. & Ocasio, W. (1999). 'Institutional logics and the historical contingency of power in organizations: executive succession in the higher education publishing industry 1958–1990'. *American Journal of Sociology,* 105, 801–843.

Tjosvold, Dean (1984). 'Effects of crisis orientation on managers' approach to controversy in decision making'. *Academy of Management Journal,* 1984, 27(1), 130–138.

Trochim, William M. K. & Donnelly, James P. (2007). *The Research Methods Knowledge Base.* 3rd Edn. Mason, OH: Atomic Dog.

Trull, Samuel G. (1966). 'Some factors involved in determining total decision success'. *Management Science,* 12(6), 270–280.

Turner, B. (1976). 'The organisational and inter-organisation development of disasters'. *Administrative Science Quarterly,* 21, 378.

Tversky, A. & Kahneman, D. (1974). 'Judgment under uncertainty: heuristics and biases'. *Science*, 185. 1124–1131.

Tversky, Amos; Kahneman, Daniel (1986). 'Rational choice and the framing of decisions'.The *Journal of Business*, 59(4/2), S251–S278.

University of Washington. (2011). 'Clawbacks make CEOs more accountable for firm's financial reporting'. http://www.foster. washington.edu/centers/facultyresearch/Pages/clawbacks.aspx.

Useem, M., Cook, J. & Sutton, L. (2005). 'Developing leaders for decision making under stress: wildland firefighters in the south canyon fire and its aftermath'. *Academy of Management Learning & Education*, 4(4), 461–485.

Vancil, Richard F. (1987). *Passing the Baton*. Harvard Business School Press.

Vaughan, D. (1996). *The Challenger Launch Decision: Risky Technology, Culture and Deviance at NASA'*. Chicago: University of Chicago Press.

Von Neumann, J. & Morgenstern, O. (1944). *Theory of Games and Economic Behavior*. Princeton, NJ: Princeton University Press.

Washington Post. (2011). 'Obama proposes higher taxes for wealthy to fund Jobs bill', http://www.washingtonpost.com/politics/obama-proposes-higher-taxes-for-wealthy-to-fund-jobs-bill/2011/09/12/gIQADrU3NK_story.html.

Walsh, I. J. & Bartunek, J. M. (2011). 'Cheating the rates: organizational foundings in the wake of demise'. *Academy of Management Journal*, 54 (5), 1017–1044.

Webb, E. (1994). 'Trust and Crisis'. In R. Kramer, & T. Tyler. *Trust in Organizations*. Newbury Park, CA: Sage.

Weick, Karl E. (1979) [1969]. *The Social Psychology of Organizing*. New York: Random.

Weick, Karl E. (1987), 'Organizational culture as a source of high reliability', *California Management Review*, 29(2), 112–127.

Weick, Karl E. (1988), 'Enacted sensemaking in crisis situation', *Journal of Management Studies*, 25(4), 305–317.

Weick, Karl E. (1989). 'Theory construction as disciplined imagination', *Academy of Management Review*, 14(4), 516–531.

Weick, Karl. E. (1990). 'The vulnerable system: an analysis of the Tenerife air disaster'. *Journal of Management*, 16(3), 571–593.

Weick, Karl E. (1993). 'The collapse of sensemaking in organizations: the Mann Gulch disaster'. *Administrative Science Quarterly*, 38, 628–652.

Weick, Karl E. (1996). 'Prepare your organization to fight fires'. *Harvard Business Review*, 74(3), 143–148.

Weick, Karl E. (2001). *Making Sense of the Organization*. Oxford: Blackwell Publishing.

Weick, Karl. E. (2007). 'The generative properties of richness'. *Academy of Management Journal*, 50(1), 14–19.

Weick, Karl. E. (2010). 'Reflections on enacted sensemaking in the Bhopal disaster'. *Journal of Management Studies*, 47(3), 537–550.

Weick, Karl. E. & Roberts, K. H. (1993). 'Collective mind in organizations: heedful interrelating on flight decks'. *Administrative Science Quarterly*, 38, 357–381.

Weick, K. E., Sutcliffe, K. M. & Obstfeld, D. (1999). 'Organizing for high reliability: processes of collective mindfulness'. In R. S. Sutton and B. M. Staw (Eds.). *Research in Organizational Behavior*, vol. 1. Stanford: Jai Press.

West, M. A. & Anderson, N. R. (1996). 'Innovation in top management teams'. *Journal of Applied Psychology*, 81, 680–93.

Westphal, J. D. (1998). 'Board games: how CEOs adapt to increases in structural board independence from management'. *Administrative Science Quarterly*, 43, 511–537.

Westphal, J. D. & Bednar, M. (2005). 'Pluralistic ignorance in corporate boards and firms' strategic persistence in response to low firm performance'. *Administrative Science Quarterly*, 50, 262–298.

Westphal, J. D., Boivie, S. & Chng, H. (2006). 'The strategic impetus for social network ties: how strategic dependencies affect the likelihood of reconstituting broken CEO friendship ties to executives of other firms'. *Strategic Management Journal*, 27, 425–445.

Westphal, J. D. & Khanna, P. (2003). 'Keeping directors in line: Social distancing as a control mechanism in the corporate elite'. *Administrative Science Quarterly*, 48, 361–398.

Westphal, J. D. & Stern, I. (2006). 'The other pathway to the board-room: how interpersonal influence behavior can substitute for elite credentials and demographic majority status in gaining access to board appointments'. *Administrative Science Quarterly*, 51, 169–204.

Westphal, J. D. & Stern, I. (2007). 'Flattery will get you everywhere (especially if you are a male Causasian): how ingratiation, board-room behavior, and demographic minority status affect additional board appointments at U.S. companies'. *Academy of Management Journal*, 50, 267–288.

Westphal, J. D. & Zajac, E. J. (1994). 'Substance and symbolism in CEOs' long-term incentive plans'. *Administrative Science Quarterly*, 39, 367–390.

Westphal, J. D. & Zajac, E. J. (1998). 'Symbolic management of stockholders: corporate governance reforms and shareholder reactions'. *Administrative Science Quarterly*, 43(1), 127–153.

Westphal, J. D. & Zajac, E. J. (2001). 'Decoupling policy from practice: the case of stock repurchase programs'. *Administrative Science Quarterly*, 46(2), 202–255.

Whitley, R. & Kristensen, P. H. (1997). *Governance at work*. Oxford: Oxford University Press.

Wheelan, Susan. (2009). 'Group size, group development, and group productivity'. *Small Group Research*, 40, 247.

Williamson, Oliver E. (1975). *Markets and Hierarchies: Analysis and Anti-trust Implications: A Study in the Economics of Internal Organization*. New York: Free Press.

Williamson, Oliver E. (1985). *The Economic Institutions of Capitalism*. New York: Free Press.

Winter, S. (1990). 'Survival, selection and inheritance in evolutionary theories of organization'. In J. V. Singh (Ed.) *Organizational Evolution: New Directions*. Newbury Park, CA: Sage Publications.

Yin, Robert K. (1994). *Case Study Research. Design and Methods*. London: Sage Publications.

Yin, Robert K. (2003). *Case Study Research: Design and Methods*. London: Sage Publications.

Zahra, S. A. & Pearce, J. A. (1989). 'Boards of directors and corporate financial performance: a review and integrative model'. *Journal of Management*, 15, 291–334.

Zajac, Edward & Westphal, J. D. (1995). 'Accounting for the explanations of CEO compensation: substance and symbolism'. *Administrative Science Quarterly*, 40(2), 283–308.

Zajac, Edward J. & Westphal, James D. (1996). 'Director reputation, CEO-board power, and the dynamics of board interlocks'. *Administrative Science Quarterly*, 41, 507–529.

Index

Business
Publishing

IE Business School is one of the world's leading institutions dedicated to educating business leaders.

IE Business Publishing and Palgrave Macmillan have launched a collection of high-quality books that give executives, students, management scholars and professionals direct access to the most valuable information and critical new arguments and theories in the fields of Business and Management, Economics and Finance from the leading experts at IE Business School.

For further information: **www.ie.edu/ie-publishing**

Also available:

Beyond Tribalism: Managing Identities in a Diverse World
978-0-230-27694-9

The Executive Guide to Corporate Restructuring
978-1-137-38935-0

Islamic Economics and Finance: A European Perspective
978-0-230-30027-9

Islamic Finance in Western Higher Education: Developments and Prospects
978-1-137-26368-1

The Learning Curve: How Business Schools Are Re-inventing Education
978-0-230-28023-6

The Long Conversation: Maximizing Business Value from Information Technology Investment
978-0-230-29788-3

Simply Seven: Seven Ways to Create a Sustainable Internet Business
978-0-230-30817-6

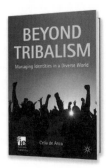

www.palgrave.com
www.ie.edu/ie-publishing

Printed and bound by CPI Group (UK) Ltd, Croydon, CR0 4YY